Marrying ApParent

A Roadmap for the Journey of Marrying a Parent

Marrying ApParent

A Roadmap for the Journey of Marrying a Parent

Erica Grace
Founder of *Marrying ApParent*

Marrying ApParent: A Roadmap for Navigating the Journey of Marrying a Parent

To protect the privacy of certain individuals who the author describes herein, their names, physical characteristics, and other identifying details have been changed. This book is designed to provide general educational information about the subjects discussed and not to diagnose, treat, cure, or prevent any physical, psychological, or emotional condition. It is not intended as a substitute for any diagnosis or treatment recommended by the reader's psychologist, psychiatrist, therapist, or medical practitioner, or for legal or spiritual advice. Use of this book does not establish any relationship between the reader and the author or publisher. Neither the publisher nor the author shall be liable for any physical, psychological, emotional, financial, legal, or commercial damages, including, but not limited to, special, incidental, consequential, or other damages resulting from the use of this book. Please be aware that references to other sources are provided for informational purposes only and do not constitute an endorsement of those sources. The advice and strategies contained herein are based on the author's personal thoughts and are not intended to be a definitive set of instructions. The reader may discover there are other methods and materials to accomplish the same result and should consult with a suitable professional when appropriate.

While the publisher and author have used their best efforts in preparing this book, they make no representations or warranties with respect to the accuracy or completeness of the contents of this book and specifically disclaim any implied warranties of merchantability or fitness for a particular purpose.

ISBN 979-8-218-51075-6 (print)

Cover Design: Everybody Eats Holdings

Contents

I dedicate this book to my children, Lucas and Sloan. Your resilience and love has not only allowed me to finish this book, but hearing you say "Marrying ApParent" throughout the house has been the equivalent of God's confirmation. To the stepparents, I hear you, I see you, I give you a voice.

"Turn your suffering into service. When you're in the moments of suffering, it gives you empathy because you sympathize with others, but then you want to turn that moment into a story that leads to service."

—David Brooks

INTRODUCTION

This book is going to ruffle some feathers. Ask me if I care. I don't! I have talked to so many people and I have learned that our situations are not that different, yet they are often kept a secret, not shared, or just too touchy to speak freely about. Conversations with stepparents and adult stepchildren planted the seed for this book. As the seed began to grow into an actual manuscript, I had the opportunity to interview dozens of parents, stepparents, couples and single people whose journeys are mapped out through these pages. Their honest, candid, and transparent interviews have been added to illustrate real experiences of people who have seriously dated or married a parent, including me.

This is a taboo subject that is so often mishandled or not handled at all. Many couples have gone through premarital counseling, but the subject of blended families and stepparenting is rarely addressed or talked about. Throughout this book is a wealth of advice and direction for people who are considering marrying a parent and those who are struggling in their marriage with a parent. You will read real-life encounters of individuals who are currently dealing with or have dealt with this topic in their lives (some names and certain details have been changed to protect their privacy). Some of what you read may be triggering, but stay present! Use this as a tool to move forward in your relationship or out of the relationship.

If you feel like you're at the end of your rope and can't take it anymore, I'm here to tell you that your marriage doesn't have to end, and neither does your engagement—you may just need to recalibrate. If you're dating, you may just need to pump the brakes to make sure that the parent you're in love with takes time to get things in order, set boundaries, and fully devote themselves to you and your union.

Use this book as a tool. You can absolutely have a beautiful, loving blended family. They exist, and you can most certainly have it! But it will require work. All things long-lasting require work. If, after you've taken all of the steps and done all of the work, you find it's still not working, be okay with walking away.

In 2018 when the idea of writing a book about being a stepmom entered into my mind, I began developing a chapter list. I started filming interviews with adult stepchildren and pondering over what this would turn into. As I was preparing to fully dive in, I became pregnant with my second child, had a challenging pregnancy, lost my job, had a baby, lived through a pandemic, got a new job, lived more life, got my dream job, and then I turned forty. This book lived in the background of my mind for five years. It was something I knew I needed to write, but I was procrastinating and letting those doubts and fears set in, and so I dragged it out until my world turned upside down—when my marriage ended.

Truth is, my marriage was laid on peat soil and bound to crumble at any moment. Peat soil is the worst foundation to build a home on because it absorbs too much water while simultaneously drying out too easily. Worse than taking too much water and then drying out too fast, peat soil is also flammable. When a home is built on a bad foundation, it shifts, it cracks, the doors and windows stop working, the entire home becomes misaligned, and eventually the home is no longer safe or stable. When a marriage is built on an unstable foundation, it shifts, hearts crack, the marriage stops working, the spouses become misaligned, and eventually the individuals within it no longer feel safe and the family is no longer stable. I attribute the weak foundation of my marriage to two things:

1) marrying a parent who had a contentious relationship with his child's other biological parent, and
2) going into the marriage deaf, dumb, and blind.

The marriage crumbled, and I take accountability for my part in its demise because I tried to build an empire on peat soil. There are a few things that kept me in the marriage longer than I should have been. One of those things was this book. Every time I'd think about leaving and getting the courage to say, "We need to talk," a small voice inside me would ask: *How can you publish a book about marrying a parent and no longer be married to a parent?* When my world turned upside down, which I'll address later on, the little voice was momentarily silenced by a bigger voice that demanded, *Get out of this marriage NOW!* That voice was loud and powerful, unable to be ignored. I listened to it.

In the midst of turmoil, I was on the phone with my brother. While we were chatting on the phone, I began talking myself out of my five-year dream of becoming an author. I felt like a fraud. How could I write a book about marrying a parent when I was about to be divorced? Now, let me make you understand something: I am a dreamer. When I was six years old and in the first grade, I said, "I want to be a lawyer when I grow up," and twenty years later, I was a lawyer. I go after what I want, so when this book entered my world, I was going to do it! So not only were pages of the book written and interviews recorded, but I'd also put it out into the ether. I didn't just talk about this dream, but on February 6, 2022, after reading a chapter in Napoleon Hill's *Think and Grow Rich*, I actually wrote it down! In Hill's self-confidence formula, which is about midway into his book, I pledged that in three years—on February 3, 2025, to be exact—I'd achieve freedom through the publication of my book. It was already manifested. How can a dreamer turn away from manifestation?

So, in the midst of me talking myself out of writing, with the little voices dancing around like sugarplum fairies, God hit me in the back of the head with the Rafiki stick (watch Disney's *The Lion King* if you don't get the reference). Then, I heard Him speak to me in an extremely loud voice. He said, *NO, ERICA, YOU AREN'T A FRAUD—YOU'RE A SOURCE.*

I paused, because I immediately received this information. My hardship made my story more honest, fair, and trustworthy, because I had gone from a single person dating a parent to a stepparent and finally to a solo parent. Now, the words that I had written as a frustrated spouse and stepmom would become my motivation, my service, my journey. Instead of just advising people who have children on how to be equitable to their partners and spouses, I got to take my own advice and test it out. This process meant I would get to prove that how I felt when I was a married wife of two children and a bonus child still resonated now that I was a divorced solo parent.

There is a quote that was taken from a few different sources and combined to loosely say: When the student is prepared, the teacher will emerge. When the student is fully prepared, the teacher will fade away. Some believe the teacher disappears because the lesson is learned, but maybe instead, you simply transition from the role of the student to the role of the teacher. As a student, this idea of *Marrying ApParent* was placed on my heart. The teacher had appeared on many occasions and encouraged me to write, but I had not been ready during our first encounter five years ago. But once I knew I was ready to publish this, the teacher disappeared and left the chalk on my nightstand when she went.

"The way of a fool seems right to them, but the wise listen to advice."[1] Looking back, there were several red flags, stop signs, rumble strips, and closed roads that ultimately led to my divorce. But all these devices meant to make me stop, slow down, and proceed with caution ultimately allowed me to write a well-rounded book with true experiences. My hope is that with this book, we can go through the *Marrying ApParent* (MAP) journey together. My hope for you is this: date with intention, set boundaries, give stepparents a voice, and

1 Proverbs 12:15 (NIV).

create a healthy environment for both yourself and your partner.

Below is a glossary of terms you'll see me use often:

- **COBP:** Child's other biological parent, i.e. the person that the parent had a child with.
- **Parent:** Someone who is coming into a relationship with a child or children from a previous relationship.
- **Single:** Someone with no children who is currently dating or entering a relationship with a parent.

Marrying ApParent has taken on the acronym MAP, which is fitting, because a map is a symbolic depiction emphasizing relationships between elements of some space, such as objects, regions, or themes. *Marrying ApParent* is a roadmap that depicts relationships between people and gives them tools to navigate these special connections. Maps have elements. A few of those elements are direction, symbols, and legends. At the end of each chapter, there is a MAP Title, MAP Legend, and MAP Directions.

On a map, the title is important because it gives the viewer a succinct description of the subject matter of the map. Here, you will get a concise point or rule that summarizes the subject matter of the chapter with the MAP Title. The legend is the key to understanding the map and, together with the title, is the first place you should look when reading a map. You should use the MAP Legend as a roadmap to understand the key points of each chapter. Direction on a map, established by a compass showing north, south, east, and west, is the way that you have to travel to get from one place or object to another place or object. Here, the MAP Directions are questions to ask when you're becoming involved in what could evolve into a co-parenting situation. Use these questions to steer conversations and allow them to help you ask uncomfortable questions to both your partner and yourself. These questions are conversation starters that should help you begin to navigate the direction you want to go in with your partner.

Last thing: *Marrying ApParent* is your guide or roadmap to navigating serious issues, questions, conversations and finding joy with your partner. The product of these conversations will be a strong infrastructure that can uphold a fulfilling, loving marriage. This ain't meant to be easy—*Marrying ApParent* is a bootcamp! Don't be afraid of the book. Don't be afraid of encounters. Don't be afraid to say hard things. Lean in. Love hard. And get your shit in order before you say, "I do," because marriage is not as apparent when marrying a parent. In fact, it's hard as fuck! Are you ready?

Chapter 1: Dating a Parent

There is nothing simple about dating a parent or dating when you have children. For the parent, it means making time for this wonderful process. It means—like everything else in your busy life—carving out time, putting it in your schedule, and shutting everything else down while you're on a date, including the kids. For the single person who doesn't have children (we will call them "the singles" throughout this book), it means having the patience of Job. Not only was Job patient, but he had perseverance, endured suffering, showed great endurance, and was steadfast under intense pressure. This is what it's like dating someone with children (we will call them "the parent")—minus the suffering. Do not date *anyone* where suffering is part of the equation.

According to Britannica.com, a nuclear family is a group of individuals connected by partnership and parenthood, typically comprising two adults and their biological children. While the adults in a nuclear family are usually married, this is not always the case.[2] Some of us grew up in or have idolized the traditional "nuclear" family, but those days (for many) are long gone. There is an upward trend of solo parent households. According

---

2 "Nuclear Family," *Encyclopædia Britannica,* accessed August 25, 2024, https://www.britannica.com/topic/nuclear-family.

to the Pew Center for Research, the number of single father households has grown nearly nine times since 1960, rising from fewer than 300,000 to over 2.6 million by 2011. During the same period, single mother households saw more than a fourfold increase, reaching 8.6 million in 2011, up from 1.9 million in 1960. In 1960, fathers led about 14% of single-parent households; today, they head almost one-quarter (24%) of these households.[3] What this means is that the odds that a solo parent might be in your dating profile and portfolio are increasing. Have an open mind, understand the new dynamics, and embrace what your family might look like one day. If any of these statistics bother you, or if you're stuck in the 1950s, close this book and go find someone who doesn't have children. If you're still here, let's learn together!

Dating a parent means that you're okay beginning a relationship with someone who has different priorities. Dating someone with children means understanding that they aren't available at your beck and call and they really don't have time for games, because they barely have time at all. It also means that, unless they have an extremely active, understanding, and engaging co-parent or village, spontaneity is pretty much impossible.

On the other hand, if you're a parent, you may have to relearn how to date. Learn yourself, know what to look out for in a partner, and use the Marrying ApParent Titles (MAP Titles) in this book as a tool to spot any issues that would be counterproductive to

---

[3] Gretchen Livingston, "The Rise of Single Fathers," Pew Research Center, July 2, 2013, https://www.pewresearch.org/social-trends/2013/07/02/the-rise-of-single-fathers/#fn-17500-1.

your lifestyle with your children. If you're single, learn about the solo parent you're dating. Take some time to understand how they show up in the lives of their children. Have patience with the solo parent and grasp their dynamic as an individual.

A SINGLE MAN DATING A SOLO MOM: KAN

Kan is a forty-three-year-old single man living in New York City. Kan has no children and because Kan prefers to date a woman in his age range, he is in a pool full of women who have children. One day, Kan was chatting with some friends and expressed how difficult it is dating a woman with children. One of the friends that knew I was writing this book urged Kan to call me, and he did. I spoke with Kan to understand his perspective. I jumped right in and asked, "What is the most difficult thing about dating a woman with children?" Kan immediately responded: "It's annoying!" I laughed. While many solo mamas may have been taken aback or even offended by Kan's response, I was not. As I listened to Kan, it dawned on me that this was about to be a great learning moment for many newly single parents, including myself.

First, Kan explained that it was hard to meet up with the woman he was dating. He explained that her child's father was inactive, and so doing anything spontaneous was out the window. He said that the extra levels of planning made it more work when he was trying to figure out when he could see her or take her out on a date. Kan also explained that even speaking to the woman was annoying because she always had something going on in the background: "Either she is talking to her kid [or] doing homework with her kid, and I swear every three minutes she tells me to hold on."

As I listened, I pictured the mom Kan was dating. I *was* her! Not that I was dating, but I was juggling a career, two children, trying to squeeze in phone calls with friends and family, and trying to find a quiet moment for myself along the way. Kan continued, "When she gets back on the line, she wants to continue the conversation like nothing ever happened. I just can't stand it." Kan's date needed to make time to date Kan. As a single mama, perhaps, she didn't understand that dividing her time and attention between her kids and Kan (at the same damn time) meant neither one of them was getting quality time. Kan's fury made me laugh, but I totally understood because once upon a time, I was a single girl with no kids who had besties with children.

My friends and I went from chatting on the phone around the clock with no distractions to multiple distractions because littles ones were always crying, talking, or asking for something. To this day, one of my girlfriends will tend to her child in the middle of me talking and then come back on the line and say in a monotone voice, "Ga 'head," as if she didn't just interrupt me mid-cry while dealing with a tragedy. I hated it then, and even though I have two children of my own, I hate it now. The difference is, now I get it, because I do the same thing (minus the monotone "Ga 'head"). As a matter of fact, one of my besties and I chat quite frequently and have incorporated the background noise of toddler cries, autistic stimming, video games, questions, and random disciplining into our conversations. Yet, with all of the racket in the backdrop, we still somehow manage to have meaningful dialogue, laughs, and mainly compassion for one another and each other's surroundings and environments. Because we are parents, we also know when to tell each other to "go and handle dem babies" when we can see the other one is spent or has no more capacity for the energy on the other line. We take no offense and make no qualms about a deep conversation coming to an abrupt halt because we understand our world, the world of a parent.

I was unexpectedly able to experiment and use some of Kan's experience in my own life. I met someone through mutual friends a few months after interviewing Kan. We looked at each other across the table and I was immediately attracted to him, and apparently he felt the same, because he asked me to dance. We danced and vibed all night, and before leaving, he asked for my phone number. The next day, he texted me and told me how much of a pleasure it was to meet me. I told him to call me sometime (because I'm a forty-one-year-old millennial who refuses to get to know someone by text only). He asked if he could call me that evening, and with Kan's advice in mind, I asked my dance partner to call me after 8:30 p.m. because I knew my children would be asleep.

At 8:30 p.m., with a quiet apartment and a bit of anticipation, my phone rang. We chatted about the weekend, asked each other questions to start to get to know one another, and during this conversation, within the first twenty minutes or so, I told him about my two children. I knew it was something I needed to be upfront about early. I paused. This was a first for me, and I must say, it was very uncomfortable. I did not know what to expect in this new space and to be honest, the first few months after my separation, being a single mom felt like a flaw that no man could or would ever look past. I wondered who would want this single mom of two.

Without hesitation, he responded, "That's love," and I silently exhaled. We continued the conversation with ease, and later he asked, "How do you find time to date while being an executive, a professor, and a mom?" I thought it was an excellent question, and thanks to Kan, I was prepared to answer it. I told him that he was the first person that I had exchanged numbers with after my divorce, and although this was new, I was intentionally making time for it.

A SINGLE GIRL AND A NONCUSTODIAL DAD: TOM

I once casually dated a noncustodial parent. The guy—let's call him Tom—had his son *maybe* every other weekend, and on those weekends when I wanted to hang out, Tom sent his son to his parents' house. Looking back with my 20/20 hindsight, there is no way in the world he should have been going out on dates with me when his son was in his custody. His time with his son was supposed to be just that—his time with his son. If it was a one-off, like a wedding or a birthday or a Beyoncé concert, then it would be understandable, but it wasn't a one-off. This was Tom's norm and who he was as a dad. As a parent myself now, I am pretty sure that this is not the best way to show up for your child. Tom was not handling dating and parenting very well.

Now, let's not blame the parent here! Part of dating is assessing your partner, who they are, and how they show up in their roles. Being a parent is a major part of a person's identity, and if you're dating a parent and they're showing you that they aren't active with their child, you must take some accountability and make better choices. Yes, it was Tom's job to be present with his child, but it was also my responsibility to tap into what was happening with Tom, myself, and his son. Why was I okay with Tom spending so much time with me, and not as much time with his child? We must take accountability for the role we play in relationships, and sometimes it's hard admitting that we aren't always right. I was wrong. Tom and I were casual. I never met his son and never intended to, but this was my chance and my responsibility to peek into his fatherhood window and identify that something was off. I should have spotted the red flag, and that was my error. In the end, our collection of colorful red, yellow, and green flags that we each collected looked like the front of the United Nations. And that led to the end of us dating.

Although we weren't serious, spending time with me was taking time from his son. As a dad, Tom should have been evaluating me. How did I respond to father-son weekends? Did they register on my calendar? Did I care? Did I allow them to bond, or did I interrupt? It was Tom's job to make sure I respected his role as a father. At the time, I was clueless. I didn't have children, so I didn't know better. But what did Tom do? He ignored my selfishness and shirked his responsibilities as a dad.

DATING & MARRYING A CUSTODIAL PARENT

Marjorie, a thirty-year-old professor, married her husband, Daniel. Daniel was the extremely available noncustodial parent. Like many of us, Marjorie thought it was amazing that her partner had so much time for her, even when his daughters were in his custody. She experienced shell shock after their wedding. Once they were in the groove of being husband and wife and parents, things shifted. Daniel's priorities quickly changed because once he got married, his ex pushed for daddy-daughter time *without* Marjorie. Because Marjorie's husband hadn't set that standard while they were dating, this new development caused a heap of trouble in their marriage.

As a single, dating a parent is understanding that they'll have background noise, be expected to spend one-on-one time with their child, have lots of priorities (many of which are unexpected) and accepting that if the child or children are young, the parent will be more heavily involved.

When you're the parent, being honest and telling someone early on that you are, in fact, a parent as well as intentionally making time to talk to them when your children are not around is a great way to make time to date. It lets the person know that not only do your children deserve your undivided attention—they do as well! With transparency, the person you are dating may be more understanding and patient with your schedule and life, and if it ever becomes too much for them, they can express it so you all can respectfully go your separate ways.

Carving out time to date is extremely important, because it will dictate how your entire relationship flows. If you're dating with marriage as the goal, you need to learn now how to juggle being a parent and a spouse. Those of us who are (or were) already married understand how crucial this is. Making time for another person allows you to be a great partner while minimizing the guilt. Intelligently dating means being extremely intentional about making time for another human and being okay with being penciled into someone's calendar.

MAP Titles:

- Parents: schedule time to date!
- Singles: be patient!
- Beware of the extremely available noncustodial parent.

MAP Legend:

- A noncustodial parent who only sees their child every other weekend should *not* be spending time with you when they have their child.
- Spontaneity might not be possible when dating a custodial parent.
- Patience is paramount when dating a parent.

MAP Directions:

- Are you the custodial or noncustodial parent?
- How often do you see your child/children?
- How do you make time to date while being a parent and juggling your priorities?

Chapter 2: Co-Parent or Show Parent

When I got married, I was a single girl with no children. My ex had a daughter from a previous relationship. I had nieces and nephews and godchildren and yes, they're my babies, but auntie responsibilities do not compare to having children of your own (unless you're raising them under your roof). Now, with almost eight years in the mommyhood, I understand that children are a 24/7/365 **JOB WITH NO DAYS OFF**. From the moment they take their first breath, you're theirs: to have and to hold, for better or for worse, for richer and for poorer, in sickness and in health, in the morning and at night, when they're newborns, teenagers, and parents themselves, forsaking rest and sleep as you once knew it as long as you both shall live. Ain't no breaks!

FINANCIALLY RESPONSIBLE: SHAUN & TAKEYA

Shaun is one of the singles I interviewed, and he is a noncustodial dad dating a custodial mom. Shaun and Takeya have been dating for about nine months. Takeya has a six-year-old boy and Shaun has a four-year-old little girl who lives in another state. When I sat down to talk with Shawn and share the *Marrying ApParent* brand with him, he was quite intrigued. I asked if his girlfriend had met his daughter yet, and he said no. I asked if he would allow his daughter's mom to meet his girlfriend before his daughter, and he replied, "Yes, that's only right." I then asked if he had met his girlfriend's son. He said yes. I asked whether he'd met the father, and he said no. I gave him the side-eye and he chuckled. He went on to explain that the little boy's father was incarcerated and they would likely never meet. As we continued to chat, I asked how he felt about taking care of his girl and her son. He stopped and reflected for a moment. He said that it dawned on him that if he was going to date a woman with a child who had an absent father, he was signing up to be this kid's dad, and he was 100% correct.

If you marry a custodial parent, you'll have the same vows that the parent you're marrying has with their kid, because they will be yours as well—emotionally, mentally, and financially. Think about this as you consider marrying a parent, especially a custodial parent, because there are NO breaks! If you date a custodial parent, you will become an instant parent. The younger the child is, the more involved you will be, and the less involved the other parent is, the more involved you will be. In this instance, Shaun was signing up to be a full-time custodial parent to his girlfriend's son.

Now, "noncustodial" doesn't mean you're on vacation from parenting or that you get to pretend you don't have children. By definition, a noncustodial parent is a parent who doesn't have physical custody of their minor child. Rarely do I see a 50/50 arrangement, but now that I'm on the other side, it's pure bullshit for it to be anything but 50/50. Sharing custody 50/50 with your COBP may not mean that they are at each parent's home 182.5 days out of the year. But what it should mean is that each parent is there 100% of the time to pick up the slack and be a parent when the other one cannot.

I'm a contract lawyer with a type B personality. I'm able to remove emotion from arrangements that are businesslike in nature. Having to deal with an ex-spouse or partner where the relationship ended the way ours did, I thought it would be best to treat things extremely black-and-white. "Black-and-white" for my lawyer brain means putting things in an agreement and moving on through there. Before I filed for divorce, I thought about how we could best show up collaboratively for our children. I remembered watching a show on Netflix where the couple divorced but had a bird's nest custody arrangement.

A bird nesting divorce or bird's nest custody allows children to stay in the family home and spend time with each parent. According to Maddy Savage in an article she wrote for the BBC entitled "Birdnesting: The divorce trend where parents rotate homes," birds-nesting is a post-divorce arrangement where the children remain in a single home and each parent takes turns living there during their scheduled parenting time, residing elsewhere when it's the other parent's turn. The term comes from the way bird parents care for their chicks, taking turns staying in the nest to ensure their safety.[4] When children are with either parent, they're always in their own beds. Although the inconvenience falls on the parent, I didn't mind that.

---

[4] Maddy Savage, "Birdnesting: The divorce trend where parents rotate homes," BBC, August 5, 2021, https://www.bbc.com/worklife/article/20210804-birdnesting-the-divorce-trend-in-which-parents-rotate-homes.

The kids didn't ask for any of this, so they should be the least disrupted. Birdnesting meant that whenever Dad wanted to spend time with the kids, I would leave the marital home, and he'd stay in the "bird's nest" with the children. To me, this arrangement seemed like something that would be best for the children. They'd have all of their things (beds, toys, and clothes) in one location and wouldn't become weekend nomads.

Unfortunately, their dad vehemently opposed the idea—not because he thought it wouldn't be good for the kids, but because, in his words, "I'm not sleeping there once I move out." In my mind, that would've been the best option, and I always gave him the option to see these beautiful kids daily! I was never ever going to be the type of mom who kept the kids away from their father. I let it go. I've come to understand that you have to relinquish some levels of control once you separate from your COBP. Unless it is for the protection of a child's mental and/or physical safety, children should have access to both of their parents. I understand some people have to make that call for safety reasons, but that should be the ONLY reason why a parent makes the decision to keep their children away from their other biological parent. Just because someone might not be the best spouse doesn't mean they won't be the best parent. Children should have full access to both parents, and parents should have full access to their kids.

Despite many difficult events that occurred after our separation, I have maintained compassion for my ex-husband. I was in love with him, had children with him, and built a life with him. So, despite the uncomfortable things that I will share here (and so much I have chosen not to share), in my optimistic mind, the potential flexibility of our arrangement means that although the children are with me more now, it's okay for things to change down the road. Just because he did not grow in his role as a husband to me doesn't mean that he can't mature and become the most active dad in the world.

Or does it?

Had I read a book on marrying a parent eight years ago, I would've been able to answer that question without rose-colored glasses. You see, it's extremely important to know what you're getting yourself into, and that comes from observing with all three eyes: the two on your face, and the one on your forehead> . . . your mind's eye (aka your intuition). Your intuition feels and senses when something is off. You can ask lots of questions, but people—especially manipulative people—can become pros at giving answers that sound good. In addition to asking difficult and uncomfortable questions, you must observe behaviors! Observing human behavior takes a lot of time, which is why marrying a parent is nothing to rush into. See, when you're dating someone, they're going to put on a show to prove that they're an awesome parent. Pay attention and take your time to decide if you're dating a "show parent" or a co-parent.

Let me give you an example. Think about the best mom or dad that you know. Not someone in their fifties and beyond, but someone between the age of twenty-five and forty-five, the social media generation. Do you have the person in your head? Ok, now ask yourself this: "How often do I see ________ post their child or children on social media?" Now, an active custodial 24/7/365 parent is not posting their crumb snatchers on social media all day, every day. You know why? They're too busy parenting! You might see a post on their birthday, the first day of school, Kwanzaa, Chanukah, Christmas, Diwali, their 100th day on the earth, a few other holidays here and there, prom, and maybe any vacations, but not every single day.

Notice the patterns. For example, if you see a parent who posts their kids on a random weekend doing nothing or notice some other kind of pattern—like they only post the kids every other weekend or something like that—you better take note. If you didn't know that a person had a child until Mother's Day or Father's Day, you better believe they are a show parent, and you do not want to marry someone who displays that type of behavior.

What is a "show parent," you ask? It's someone who is with their kids for show. Maybe they show up when their son has a championship football game, or their daughter is accepting an award in college. Perhaps they're unavailable all summer long to help share childcare responsibilities, but they make sure they're there on the first day of school to walk their children to their homeroom. You have some people who don't see their children very often, but they are all over social media with the deepest quotes and captions. It's optics. It's a show, and they're LYING! They eat up all of the comments under the pictures and convince themselves that they are the best parent in the world. Don't date the show, and damn sure don't marry the show. This is not authentic parenting! The farce is indicative of how they will show up in real life. Just like the Instagram story, their parenting will be limited to twenty-four hours, or the high holidays and you'll be parenting alone, whether you're married to them or divorced from them.

There are many noncustodial parents who are in their child's lives daily. "Noncustodial" doesn't equate to "inactive." A person can be a noncustodial parent and still be a damn good parent by simply always making themselves available to their children. If the child has a school event, they're present. Class trip? They're volunteering. Kid is sick and the custodial parent took off the last three times? The noncustodial parent is taking off the fourth time. The child may not live with them, but if the kids need them 24/7/365, they're there. This is the kind of noncustodial parent you want to date and marry. This is a co-parent. A true co-parent doesn't use their noncustodial status as a "get out of parenting free" card; they're there *all the time* for their child.

COURTING A SHOW PARENT: ART & YOLI

Art was smitten with his new girl, Yoli. He raved about Yoli and mentioned that she had a son. Art said when he walked into her home, Yoli had twenty-foot pictures of her children on the walls of her loft and boasted about her son's Division 1 basketball career and deals that were starting to be presented by his coach. I asked Art questions and learned that Yoli wasn't raising her son. She became pregnant in her first year of college. Her mom had taken care of her grandson so her daughter could remain on campus and get the full college experience. Once she graduated, she moved to New York City and although she had the space and financial means to take care of her child, she left him behind.

Her son, now seventeen, was doing extremely well in basketball. She made sure his pictures were all over her social media and her home, but she had never mothered her son. To my friend who hadn't been dating her very long, she looked like an active mom, but after some tough questions it dawned on him that he was dating a show parent.

My ex-husband talked about his child often. He gave me tidbits and anecdotal stories of conversations with his daughter and oh, it was just too cute. He'd send pictures of them together every now and then, and I ate it up. At the time, he didn't have a custody arrangement with his COBP or consistent parenting time, but once we got married, I made sure he went to court so that he could have consistent parenting time. He took her to and from school, I did homework with her, and she was woven into the fabric of our new blended family.

At the time, I did not mind stepping up, but looking back it should have been handled before he even began dating. It's not your place to demand, ask, force, or even gently nudge the person you're dating to go to court for custody or parenting time with their child. That is not your responsibility. It should never take a third party to come into your life to make you be a better parent, because once they're gone, what's causing you to still show up? Nothing! Moving forward, I wouldn't date a noncustodial parent who doesn't already have a clear schedule for seeing their child or children. If you marry a show parent, grab your popcorn and prepare to be entertained.

MAP Title: Don't date or marry a show parent.

MAP Legend:

- Pay attention to what the parent is doing instead of what they are saying.
- Marrying a custodial parent means you instantly become a parent as well.
- A true noncustodial parent is someone who is consistently present for their child.

MAP Directions:

- **Noncustodial:**
    - What days is your child with you?
    - Do you and the COBP take turns caring for your child outside of parenting time?
    - If your child is sick, who takes off work?
    - Will dating me cause any issues with your current arrangement?
- **Custodial:**
    - Why doesn't the other parent see the child/children more frequently?
    - Do you think you've done anything to prevent them from seeing each other more often?

Chapter 3: Boundaries

The truth is: Stepparenting is hard, no matter who you are in the relationship, what created the situation you're in, or where you are on the spectrum, from easy (all parties, biological parents, and stepparents get along and are able to communicate well) to difficult (the courts have to make all of the decisions regarding what goes on in your household with your stepchild). The main reason it's hard is because your spouse's ex (or a person they've been intimate with and made a child with) is always around. When you break up with a significant other who you have no children with, it's a clean break. You no longer talk to them, your relationships with their friends and family slowly fade to black, and you completely disconnect from them. When a child is involved, though, there is no disconnection. This person, their spirit, their ideals, and their influence over your partner is loud unless you're with a partner who knows how to silence the noise.

As I sit here, transparently and candidly, I have to painfully admit that my motivation to write again came from a violation of epic proportions. Let me set the stage for you: When I met my ex-husband, he was no longer with the COBP. There had been a separation, and he'd had another relationship after the relationship with his COBP ended and ours began. I figured it would be smooth sailing, but I wasn't privy to a lot of the mess until it was too late. I did not know that the relationship I was journeying into was limitless and open like outer space, and as capacious as it was, there was no space for me. I didn't perceive the relationship as roomy and free; to me, it felt claustrophobic, suffocating, and extremely isolating.

You see, some people perceive boundaries as walls. They feel boxed in when boundaries are set because disorderly people struggle with structure. Systems are necessary for most people—for disorderly individuals, but especially for people who want to be healthy. Lack of organization is confining and confusing because the line is always moving. I felt restricted within the bounds of their old relationship because my ex-husband never set the stage for a new one. My ex-husband's failure to set boundaries in life caused me to be stuck in a situation that I never was meant to be a part of, and oh, would that theme play over and over again throughout our eight-year relationship.

Boundaries are necessary in all aspects of life because they set the standard of how you'll operate. When you're looking for a new job, you know what you want. You know the salary requirements that you need. You know whether you're flexible to being remote, hybrid, or are willing to thug it out five days per week in the office. You know when you want to shut down for the day and go see your kids or hit happy hour with your friends. You know what to wear in the office, how to effectively and respectfully communicate with your managers, and how you want those managers to communicate with you. If you're a 9-to-5er, you wouldn't expect your boss to ask you to come in to work at 5:00 a.m. These are all boundaries that you have set. The workplace is probably one of the easiest places to set boundaries. If you decide to wear what you wore to the beach in Cabo to the big board meeting, you know that you have crossed a boundary and might lose your job.

When I was first writing, I added a few bullets to a list called "Other Topics." One of those other topics was separation and divorce. At the time, it never dawned on me that this would become part of my story. In fact, this "other topic" has now become a major reason behind why I picked back up and started writing again. So, here goes . . .

My ex-husband had an affair with the COBP. WOOOOOOOO, there, I said it. While I was at work at my brand-new dream job, my husband had a *six-month* affair (that included dates, gifts, erotic images, and *more*) with the woman he supposedly hated. The woman who hated me. The woman who had once spewed racial slurs at me and our nieces, nephews, and later our children. The woman who withheld his child from him for months at a time on multiple occasions. The woman who, despite all of these things, was the mother of someone I loved, and because of that I love, I eventually did everything in my power to learn to tolerate and get along with. My broken heart led me here—it is THE reason why this book needs to be read and absorbed. It was betrayal soup. The combination of the lies, pain, and lack of boundaries were a clear indication to me that it was time to exit. Although the pain was unbearable and something I can't quite describe, I deeply feel that the beauty in the pain will be manifested in this: *Marrying ApParent.*

Setting and respecting boundaries won't only prevent loss of your job—it can also prevent loss of your partner. The losses that I experienced were completely preventable. So, here's some advice: Do not marry a parent who has trouble setting and sticking to boundaries. My ex-husband had ZERO boundaries in place, and the lack of respect that bled from that was the ultimate death of our marriage. Boundaries are necessary in all relationships between humans, platonic, professional, familial, and romantic. If you don't have boundaries, you have chaos. Boundaries must be honored so that people know that they are being respected. We had no boundaries.

Parents, the success of this entire process starts with you. If you want a peaceful, strong marriage and a smooth blend for your family, then this chapter is the loam soil on which to build your foundation. Loam is the best soil to build on because it blends the best attributes of silt, sand, and clay into the ultimate base for sustaining a foundation. Your most important undertaking is going to be to set very clear boundaries with the COBP. When you set clear boundaries before you even begin dating, it sets you up for success. Setting boundaries before you blend your family will allow for a smooth transition because the COBP and your child will already be accustomed to the boundaries. If you wait until you have someone new in your life to establish the parameters with the COBP, you're setting your potential partner up for failure from the onset of the relationship, because the COBP and your child will make the new person the scapegoat for the reasons why their interactions with you have changed. It shifts the accountability from you to the other person, and even if it *is* you making necessary changes, your child and COBP won't perceive it that way, and you will put your partner on the fast track for the "evil stepparent" title. By setting boundaries, you set the tone for your child, the COBP, and your spouse. Here are four boundaries that I find are important in establishing a new relationship: Meet the Parent, Communication, Good Fences, and Friendships. This is not an exhaustive list of boundaries, but it's a good start.

BOUNDARY NO. 1: MEET THE PARENT

I should have never met my stepchild before I met her mother. My ex and I crossed this boundary together. Kids are fragile, and they deserve to be handled with care. As a parent, your number one job is to protect your children. A healthy parent would never want just anybody around their child. The point of this meeting is for you and the COBP to get to know one another. The first time you meet the COBP, you're going to see and feel things that cannot be faked. Your job is to listen and observe. As the single, you want to learn about the COBP and the child, and as a natural consequence, you will also get to know more about the parent you're dating. The COBP doesn't get to determine who you date, but getting to know them will give you a window into a relationship that you know nothing about—theirs.

I can guarantee you that the vibes and energy will be extremely strong during this first meeting. The energy from the COBP is either going to give you green light or red light energy. Again, taking responsibility for my own actions, I missed this step. I crossed this crucial boundary, and it set the stage for mayhem.

Although I had no control over meeting the COBP, I did have control over meeting the child (sort of).

I remember the first time I met my stepdaughter. For some context, my ex-husband and I did not have a title at the time; we were just hanging out, but hanging out in a way that could potentially lead to a romantic partnership. On a hot summer night in August, my ex invited me to come hang out with him and his friends. The plan was to have a casual barbeque at one of his friends' homes. I was at my mom's house with the family for my sister's birthday. His plan was to leave his friend's house to take his daughter home and by the time I got to his house, he'd be back. When I pulled up to his house, he told me to walk across the park to where he was parked. I got in his car, we chatted for a bit, and his phone rang. He said he'd be right back, and as he hopped out of the car, he looked back and said, "I need to get my daughter and take her home," and nonchalantly walked off. I didn't have a moment to think, object, or ask any questions. I froze.

When you're single and young, sometimes you're just naive and stupid. Moments and actions that should make you stop talking to someone may instead feel like signs of love. "Oh my gosh . . . he trusts me enough to meet his child," naivety thinks. But experience knows that introducing someone to your child is a *big* deal, even if it is someone you are just hanging out with. Not everyone you date should have the privilege of meeting your child and being in their presence. I was not dating my ex long enough to meet his child—that was naive of me. Him casually exiting the vehicle without asking me how I felt and planning a meet up knowing that he still had to take his daughter home was selfish and inappropriate, and I was stupid to have stayed in the car. That wasn't a sign that he really liked me and it definitely did not mean I was important to him.

Don't be stupid or naive. If the person you're dating puts you in a precarious situation, open up a rideshare app and schedule a pickup. No one should be put in a situation where they do not have or cannot make a choice for themselves. I never wanted to meet my stepdaughter before I met her mother.

I remember when my stepdaughter got in the car, she was quiet and uncomfortable, and frankly, so was I. She and I had spoken on FaceTime a few times, so I tried to make small talk with this little four-year-old girl, but it was flat. I had always been so good with kids. At the time, I had three two-year-old nieces, a two-year-old nephew, and more godchildren than I could count. But this four-year-old and I were not vibing, and my ex didn't help at all. That was the longest short car ride of my life.

When we got to her home, he jumped out of the car again to take her upstairs and lo and behold, like a planned moment, the COBP pulled up next to his car. I could see her in my peripheral vision. Before I looked over, I texted him informing him that she was parked alongside me. I finally looked over and she asked me if I was Erica. She told me how much her daughter talked about me, but it was uncomfortable and awkward. He came down and got in the car, not alarmed or disturbed in the least, but I'd had no right to meet her child before I met her. Whether we were just friends, hanging out, or in a serious relationship, I should have gotten out of his car, gotten back in mine, and drove home the minute that I heard him say he had to get his child. It was a boundary that I crossed as I entered a bear's cave with a blindfold on, dangling a raw steak while attempting to take her brand new cub . . . or what some might more gently call "stepparenting."

I wished I had a rubric, some rules, Dora the Explorer's map, a mentor, anything and anybody to help me deal with my new life. Ideally, you want to have a decent, if not great, relationship with the COBP, but as a stepmama, the contention can be utterly exhausting. You want to become a team to support the child and raise them to be productive members of society. That's the goal. You as the person marrying the parent will know during the first meeting if the parent has things in order. You get to assess a whole lot during that meeting. Use it to your advantage, and don't ignore the gut reactions you have to the COBP.

MAP Title: Your COBP should meet your partner before your partner meets your child.

MAP Legend:

- Meet the parent of your potential stepchild before you meet the child.
- Observe the energy between the parent and the COBP during the meeting.

MAP Directions:

- What are your requirements before introducing someone new to your child?
- How does your COBP feel about people meeting your child?
- What do you expect from your COBP when introducing your child to someone?

BOUNDARY NO. 2: COMMUNICATION IS KEY

Communication between two people with children is essential. The frequency of communication may vary depending on the people involved—for example, it might lessen as the child enters their teen years or be less frequent if the parents have an extremely tight parenting agreement that they both adhere to strictly—but communication is a requisite. Now, the *type* of communication is where things can get wonky, and that's why boundaries in communication are important to discuss with the parent and observe on your own.

Looking at the totality of the circumstances, the communication between my ex-husband and the COBP over the eight years that we were together was frequent and inappropriate. It wasn't the frequency that made their communication inappropriate; rather, it was the fact that their relationship was laced with emotional intimacy. Licensed marriage and family therapist Beverly Engel wrote about a special closeness at the heart of emotional intimacy, a closeness that is defined by two people's mutual and deep knowledge of one another. Engel explained that emotional intimacy involves a deep level of closeness and connection between two people who feel safe and secure together. It goes beyond mere "closeness," as it includes being truly seen, known, and understood by the other person, allowing for a profound understanding of each other.[5]

---

[5] Beverly Engel, LMFT, "Emotional Intimacy: What It Is and How to Build More of It," Choosing Therapy, February 6, 2023, https://www.choosingtherapy.com/emotional-intimacy/#:~:text=Emotional%20intimacy%20is%20the%20closeness,to%20know%20each%20other%20deeply.&text=Relationships%20aren%E2%80%99t%20perfect.

Emotional intimacy is unique because it doesn't require anything tangible. It's being excited from a text message, a phone call, a glance across a room, a thought, or a simple memory. Emotional intimacy is complex, and if you have a partner who either understands your complexities or has added to them, then you have someone whom you can connect to for eternity. If the parent that you want to marry or have married has emotionally charged arguments with the COBP that have nothing to do with the child, something is wrong. Humans argue, and that is totally normal. Humans who have been in a relationship AND have children together may argue even more, and still, that is totally normal. However, when the argument is fueled by and mixed with passion, you can forget an uphill battle—you'll be climbing Mt. Everest!

MARRIED WITH A CHOKEHOLD: TAMARA & JERRY

Jerry and his wife, Tamara, fell for each other fast. They had a whirlwind romance that led to a fast marriage and a new baby Harris on the way. Jerry's son would come over every week from Thursday until Sunday. On Thursdays, everything was great—Jerry would pick his son up from school, and they'd come home and have dinner as a family. The closer it got to Sunday, though, the darker it felt in their home. Tamara couldn't put her finger on the issue until about a year into the marriage. Jerry came home after dropping his son off. When he walked into the house, he was on a call. Tamara asked who Jerry was talking to. He turned the phone around to show Tamara that he was on the phone with his son's other biological parent. Tamara mouthed,

"Put it on speaker," and when her husband shook his head no, an airless choking feeling immediately came over Tamara. Instantly, she was able to identify what was causing her house to feel disrupted every Sunday: her husband's weekly interactions with the COBP.

Her husband walked out of the kitchen into the living room and Tamara followed behind him. He sat on the couch, then she sat on the couch, trying to stay close so she could pick up a few words here and there. All of a sudden, her husband's twenty-minute silence was broken by a hearty laugh—*his* hearty laugh, followed by his snort. Jerry only snorted when something was hysterical. Tamara had always loved that snort until that moment. Tamara motioned for Jerry to hurry up and get off of the phone. Jerry looked at Tamara's worried face, got off of the couch, walked into their bedroom, and closed the door. When she went to open the bedroom door, it was locked.

Tamara lost it. She knocked on the door with an open palm, preparing herself to yell. Jerry was simultaneously opening the door, finally off of the phone, and as he emerged from the room he asked Tamara, "What's wrong with you?" Before Tamara could utter a word, Jerry began to recount parts of the conversation. Tamara—anxious, annoyed, and a little worried—asked, "What was the snort laugh about?" Jerry chuckled as he remembered the conversation and proudly said, "She told me my d*ck ruined her life," and it was at that moment that Tamara realized the COBP had a chokehold on her husband and ultimately her marriage. Jerry's conversation with the COBP not only demonstrated zero boundaries, but it was obscene, revolting, and depraved.

If you're a stepparent experiencing disrespect remotely close to what Tamara experienced, seeking a counselor is imminent, because your marriage is in grave danger and you need a hard reset. Communication between a parent and the COBP shouldn't send you sliding down a wall, experiencing a tailspin of emotions. That is a problem. It's disrespectful to you. The conversations between the parent and the COBP should be short, to the point, and about the child that they share. The only time that there should be any lengthy conversation is when there is a problem with the child; other than that, their conversations should be short and succinct. Also, anything that they're talking about, you should be privy to.

TAKE IT TO THE GROUP CHAT: LEAH & GARY

Gary has a twelve-year-old daughter with his ex-girlfriend. Before meeting his wife, Leah, Gary would communicate with the COBP in a group chat with his parents. Gary chose this method of communication because he noticed that years after their relationship ended, his COBP would text him at odd times (and too frequently), and often the texts would be about their breakup and not their parenting relationship. In order to take control of the situation and to avoid any mixed signals, Gary chose to communicate in a group chat so a third party could be witness to their exchanges. Once Leah and Gary were married, he removed his parents from the chat and added his wife to the group chat.

By setting this boundary with his ex, Gary made it clear that there wouldn't be any secrets and that he and his wife were a united front. He also protected his peace by ensuring his wife wouldn't wonder about the content of their exchanges, whether plans were being made, or whether she was being volunteered for things without having a say.

MAP Title: Set and maintain boundaries for respectful and focused communication.

MAP Legend:

- The parent must set clear boundaries on how they will appropriately communicate with the COBP.
- Communication should be clear, concise, succinct, and only about the child.
- Stepparents should be privy to all conversations taking place between the parent and the COBP.

MAP Directions:

- What is your preferred method of communication between you and your COBP?
- How do you handle contention between yourself and your COBP?
- What is the frequency of the communication between you and your COBP?

BOUNDARY NO. 3: GOOD FENCES

Boundaries play a crucial role in defining what is acceptable in any relationship—whether it is with friends, partners, colleagues, supervisors, or family members. We establish them to preserve our well-being, and they serve to promote trust, safety, and respect in our interactions.[6] It is *necessary* to have boundaries. When discussing boundaries in the workplace, Dr. Karen Otazo explained that well-defined fences set clear property lines, minimizing trespassing and ownership disputes.[7] I love this concept and will spin it for the purposes of *Marrying ApParent*: Clear lines define relationship boundaries, reducing stress and conflicts over parenting and the interactions between the parent and the COBP. Boundaries prevent the child from being used as a pawn in the relationship.

From the workplace to home, we can accept the necessity of making everyone we interact with exist between the bounds of our needs. Boundary setting, however, is not just for the parent and the COBP; it is another tool of observation for singles and stepparents. Singles, you must closely observe whether these boundaries are set, and stepparents, you MUST make sure the boundaries set in place by the parent you married are being respected, aren't crossed, and do not become moving targets. Sometimes the fences that we set around our lives change as we grow, and this is normal and expected. However, stepparents, those changes must be in synchronicity with your marriage. In my relationship, the goal was always moving. There were no boundaries in place before I began dating my ex-husband, and the boundaries that we seemed to collectively agree on

---

6 Cherrial Ann Odell, "How is Life Tree(ting) You?: Trust, Safety, and Respect - The Importance of Boundaries," Stanford Student Affairs, accessed June 3, 2024, https://studentaffairs.stanford.edu/how-life-treeting-you-importance-of-boundaries.

7 Dr. Karen L. Otazo, *The Truth About Managing Your Career ...and Nothing but the Truth* (Pearson, 2006).

as husband and wife and parents were constantly broken. As a stepmom and a wife, I should have addressed a boundary as soon as it was broken. There should have been consequences every time a line was crossed and the ultimate consequence for repeated broken boundaries has to be stepping away from the person who is constantly violating you. The best apology is changed behavior.

Boundaries that aren't established by you will be set by the law and they will be enforced by the law. Divorce decrees, parenting agreements, custody arrangements, child support, protective orders, and the like are boundaries set in place by legal authorities when the people in the situation cannot enforce or respect them themselves. If the boundaries that you've set are being completely ignored or constantly violated, it may be necessary to have a neutral party set the boundaries instead.

MAP Title: Get a third party to help set boundaries.

MAP Legend:

- You do not have to deal with constant broken boundaries.
- While dating, observe the relationship and boundaries between the parent and the COBP.

MAP Directions:

- Do you have boundaries in place with your co-parent?
- Are there any boundaries that you've set that your COBP constantly violates?
- Would you consider having a third party intervene?

BOUNDARY NO. 4: FRIENDSHIPS

Friendships between stepparents and COBP aren't only possible—they're real. Actor Orlando Bloom was married to model Miranda Kerr from 2010–2013, and they share a son, Flynn. As of this writing, Orlando is engaged to Katy Perry and they have a daughter, Daisy, together.[8] According to Miranda, they're all a "blended family" along with her husband, Evan Spiegel. On the *Moments With Candace Parker* podcast, Miranda explained that they go on vacations together and celebrate all the significant events as a unit, adding, "I love [Katy]." Miranda says that it's fair to say her love for Katy surpasses her love for Flynn's dad.

My ex-husband was not honest about his interactions with his COBP. Just to be clear, I have no issue with a parent being friends with the COBP . . . sort of. The parent and the stepparent are supposed to be best friends, confidants, and partners. Your journey together of experiencing life, hardships, love, death, job loss, raises, dream jobs, and everything in between is a journey that you're on together. Yes, you still are individuals, but every friendship that you have should be in support of your union, including any friendship with the COBP. Any friendship that doesn't support your union is a crossed boundary.

I always felt that my ex-husband was being played by his COBP. Calls disguised as being about the child became conversations about why their relationship failed. Special events like birthday parties and graduations

---

8 *CNN*, 19 August 2021, https://www.cnn.com/2021/08/19/entertainment/miranda-kerr-orlando-bloom-katy-perry-trnd/index.html. Accessed 12 August 2024.

would turn into fighting matches designed to exclude me. Ultimately, I realized that the COBP wasn't playing my ex-husband—they were collectively playing me. Although he would portray her as the villain in the story, he, in fact, had a relationship with his COBP that I knew nothing about.

When I found out about the affair, I was strangely calm yet wildly confused. The confusion was probably the most constant emotion at the time. After seven and a half years of turmoil, ups and downs, and unrest, the COBP and I were finally getting along. I remember sitting next to her at my stepdaughter's play, rubbing her arm while she cried. We were, dare I say, friendly, and I never questioned it because it was nice to see my stepdaughter happy that the adults were playing nice, and it was a breath of fresh air to finally not be at odds. I was looking forward to actually building a friendship for the sake of my stepdaughter and our future grandchildren, so the affair was shocking. To add insult to injury, the timeline of us getting along was in perfect alignment with their affair.

Affairs are hard on a marriage because being betrayed is not one emotion alone; its effects make you question whether you were ever loved, appreciated, or enough, and it shatters the trust into tiny little pieces. An affair with the COBP that you must see and communicate with while simultaneously not letting the child know what happened is not hard—it's terminating. The affair terminated our marriage, my normal weekly interaction with my stepdaughter, and any semblance of a friendship with her mom. Contentious relationships breed stress, and stress creates diseases. If you must be in a relationship, getting along in love and maintaining friendships is best. I believe it's achievable once boundaries are set and things are in order.

The parent and the COBP's friendship must be respectful. There cannot be blurred lines, flirting, or conversations about their previous relationship. It's already a weird dynamic as it is. Remember, this is not just an old friend, this is an ex—they've seen you naked, for God's sake, so I'm not saying compromise your beliefs and force a friendship "for the sake of the child." Absolutely no—fuck that! What I'm saying is, if things are in order, boundaries are set, and you actually like the COBP, then feel free to have a friendship and lead with love.

In a dream world, stepparent utopia would look like Lisa Bonet, Jason Momoa, and Lenny Kravitz's situation. In a 2020 interview with *Men's Health* magazine, Kravitz was asked about his ex-wife Lisa Bonet's then-husband, Jason Momoa. After their breakup, Kravitz noted that people are often surprised by how close he remains with both Jason and Zoë's mom. He explained that maintaining these relationships is natural and comes from a place of love. Though it requires effort, time, healing, and reflection, he and Jason instantly connected when they first met, with Kravitz thinking, "I love this dude."[9]

Friendship among co-parents, stepparents, and exes would be the most ideal situation, not only for the children but for the adults as well. Even after Lisa and Jason ended their relationship, Lenny referred

---

9 Joshua Ocampo, "Lenny Kravitz Credits Lisa Bonet With Transforming His Career," *Men's Health*, October 1, 2020, https://www.menshealth.com/entertainment/a34224654/lenny-kravitz-lisa-bonet/.

to him as his "brother for life."[10] These relationships don't only happen in Hollywood; they're real and they also happen in the lives of people we all know personally.

PARENTS & BONUS PARENTS COMMUNICATE WITH LOVE: Jeffrey and Shawn

Shawn is a pastor in Chicago, Illinois. He is a positive, likable human being, but what I appreciate most about Shawn is his honesty. He opened up to me about his relationship with his stepdaughter's dad, Jeffrey. Keshia, Shawn's stepdaughter, is thirty-seven. When I asked Shawn how he managed communication with Jeffrey over the years, Shawn said, "I loved and honored that communication because of my sincere love for Keshia. At the end of the day, I was concerned that Keshia had all of her needs met, spiritually, emotionally, physically, etc. It was a village. Additionally, I wanted to learn as much as I could regarding him [Jeffrey] and his family traits so I could identify certain traits in Keshia and could understand the genesis of those traits." In his candor, Shawn said that he supported the parenting styles of Keshia's biological parents and they had to learn to maturely work through their differences: "Love makes stepparents do the right thing."

A few days after my exchange with Shawn, Keshia and I were on our daily check-in and I asked her about

[10] Jen Abidor, "11 Times Celebs' Partners Were On SUPER Good Terms With Their High Profile Exes," Buzzfeed, September 30, 2023, https://www.buzzfeed.com/jenniferabidor/celebrities-whose-exes-are-friends-with-partners.

the relationships between her dads, and she said: "They love each other!" They crack jokes together and genuinely get along. Her words made my heart smile and confirmed that friendships can exist between stepparents and their COBPs.

MAP Title: Be honest, authentic, and respectful.

MAP Legend:

- Friendships can exist.
- If there is no trust, friendship cannot exist.
- There are no secrets between the parent and the COBP.

MAP Directions:

- How would you describe the relationship between you and your COBP?
- In an ideal world, what does the relationship look like between your COBP and the person you marry?
- How would you handle conflict between your spouse and your COBP?

Chapter 4: The Order of Things

When you grow up in a nuclear home, you learn by observation that there is an order of things: God (if you're religious), your spouse, your children, and then everyone and everything else. I have spoken to people in the Christian, Muslim, and Jewish faiths, and each have an order when it comes to parents and children. Even nonreligious married people agree their spouse comes first. The problem is that when you marry a parent, the order of things as we traditionally have come to know them is completely different. This is because the child existed prior to the partner, and ultimately the parent's new partner has to find their position in this already established familial unit.

In order to make room for the new family unit, a shift has to take place. You have to prepare your children for the shift, and the better prepared you are, the smoother the transition will be. Preparedness for singles means dating with intention, asking uncomfortable questions, understanding the parent you're dating, and holding space for the things you hold valuable as well. For a parent, preparation means taking time to date, setting and enforcing your boundaries, and having things in order like parenting time, financial obligations, and healthy communication with the COBP as well as a healthy relationship with your child.

A healthy relationship with your child means that your child understands their space in the family structure. Your child doesn't have the same position as you or their stepparent, but they still deserve respect and are allowed to have boundaries as well. The order, hierarchy, or positioning—whatever you'd like to call it—makes room for teaching, learning, structure, mistakes, correction, love, respect, and ultimately individuality and independence for your children. The goal is for the shift to be noticeable, but not catastrophic. Think breeze vs. tornado, waves vs. tsunami, flurries vs. snowstorm, drizzle vs. hurricane—you get the picture. Ideally, before a parent begins dating, there is a flow with the child that would openly hold space for the parent to have a partner.

Your children and stepchildren won't be kids forever. Author and podcast host Gretchen Rubin said, "The days are long, but the years are short," when she described the difficulty of the day-to-day of raising a child juxtaposed to how fast it goes by. Rubin is correct: The years are short and before we know it, our children will be adults, and it is our job to prepare them for their individuality while simultaneously keeping our home intact. When your child leaves the nest one day, it'll just be you and your spouse. The children are the priority to the parents as a collective, but the individuals in the marriage must also prioritize each other and their union. I know it's hard for people to fathom that their child shouldn't be their number one priority, especially when that means putting your new spouse before your child that existed before your marriage did. I get it, but what I believed during my marriage is what I believe in now: it's us vs. them. (I'm joking, but you get it!)

Your spouse should never feel like they come second to anyone. When two people come together as spouses, they are to put their marriage first. Positioning your child before your spouse can cause a feeling of separation between the child and the bonus parent, and a superficial "other family" can start to form between you, your child and the COBP. To break this down, your spouse should never feel like you have another family. Yes, you had a child or children before your spouse came into your life, and that child/children are your family. However, if you were parenting them in a healthy way, they should have never gotten the impression that they were stand-ins or placeholders for your partner, and if you're making the mistake of doing that now, stop! It's not too late to change the dynamic in your household. Once you get married, your spouse becomes your family as well, and it is your job to make sure both your child and your partner feel incorporated into the new family that you've created.

Too often, a parent will enter into a relationship or the dating game telling their potential mate, "If my child doesn't like you, then I can't be with you." Really?! How are we giving a child so much say in a major life decision? Children don't like vegetables, but I bet you feed them broccoli anyway. You have to know your child enough to be able to distinguish between manipulation and intuition. Make sure you make a distinction between a child who doesn't like broccoli and the child who is deathly allergic to it.

Children are intuitive, though, so do not ignore their feelings if they tell you that they are uncomfortable around a partner you've chosen. This is not in contradiction to what I said above. If your child feels uneasy around someone, you need to get to the bottom of it. If their reasons are any of the reasons stated below, then it may take patience and effort on your part to make both your child and your partner comfortable. However, if your child's discomfort is associated with anything inappropriate or indicates that something inappropriate could happen, kindly remove yourself and your child from that situation.

Your child might not like the person that you're dating for a few reasons. Perhaps you have allowed the child to think that their role in your life is a partnership and not a parent/child role, and they aren't prepared for the shift. Maybe you don't make time to enjoy your own company and everything is about your children, so the kids don't know how to adjust to seeing you do something for anyone else but them. Another possibility is that the COBP could be feeding your children negative information about your new partner. Lastly, they may not like your partner simply because they aren't their biological parent. All of these reasons might be true, but they aren't reason enough for you to dismiss a good person. You get to choose who you spend the rest of your life with.

Creating order in your family isn't just for the benefit of the parent–child dynamic; it is also necessary for the sibling, half-sibling, and stepsibling relationships. A child is not your partner, but your spouse is, and it is critical to have an order that makes sense for your particular family. You can create a disparate environment between your own children when you put a child over your spouse. All of your children should feel equal. When you don't make a distinction between your child's role and your spouse's role in the family, then the child(ren) that come out of your union with your new spouse won't feel equal to the child(ren) that existed from the previous relationship, and that will only result in an unbalanced disaster. Be conscious about placing children in a position where they're treated like the man of the house or forced into playing a mothering role. No child, regardless of age, should feel pressured to take care of you or stand in the same position as a partner otherwise you are dealing with an enmeshed relationship.

The term "enmeshment" was developed in the 1970s by Salvador Minuchin, who lived from 1921–2017. He was a modern psychiatrist who was one of the founding fathers of the development of family therapy. Minuchin was influential in the field of structural family therapy and introduced the concept of enmeshment. Enmeshment arises when one person's boundaries impose on others in a harmful,dependent way. With an enmeshing parent, the child's identity is dictated by the parent, who acts as if the child's actions are a reflection of themselves.[11]

A parent's job is to love their child. When a child is born, they don't know love; they only know survival. Love is either learned or not learned from the parent. If you're in a relationship with a parent who is in an enmeshed relationship with their child, you will never have an agreeable arrangement. Enmeshment can cause a divide between the children you share with your partner

---

[11] Sharie Stines, "When Narcissistic Parents have Enmeshed Boundaries with Their Children," *Psych Central,* March 11, 2020, https://psychcentral.com/pro/recovery-expert/2020/03/narcissists-have-enmeshed-boundaries-with-their-children#1.

and the child they came into the marriage with, or even worse, between you and your spouse. The relationship between the enmeshed parent and the child is highly parasitic. The parent relies on the child, who is manipulated into thinking that their sole purpose is to exist for the parent's needs[12]

This type of relationship can be seen in both mothers and fathers. If you've ever heard someone tell a young male child that he is "the man of the house" because the custodial parent is a mother, they are encouraging enmeshment. If you've ever heard a woman refer to her son as her "king," she is enmeshed with her son. How about a father who cleaves or vents to his daughter about her mother or stepmother when he's upset? What about a father who requires the eldest daughter to cook the meals or stand in to raise her younger siblings in the absence of a woman in the house? All of this behavior is out of order. A male child is not a man! He is a child, and he is certainly not your king. Your child is yours to raise (or to help raise the little unhealed child in you, according to acclaimed author and clinical psychologist Dr. Shefali), to experience, to love, but not to be in partnership with. The partner to a king is a queen, and your child shouldn't be pressured to play that role for you.

Even if you don't believe in hierarchy between parents and children, the family system must have appropriate boundaries between everyone to functionally operate. Treating your kids like your partner or the number one person in your life or fostering toxic and inappropriate enmeshment with your kids disrupts the healthy order of

---

[12] Ibid.

adult partnerships, marriage, and familial boundaries. If the idea of putting your spouse before your biological child makes you uneasy, you either don't know how to pick healthy partners or you're not ready to get married. Disorder will only cause chaos when you marry a parent.

Although your children do not get to choose your mate, your dating choices and who you bring around your children matter. You should be choosing a partner who will have a healthy impact on your children, because they will have a hand in raising them. At some point, you will realize how important it is to pick a partner who not only makes sense for you, but also makes sense for your kid. Again, I know this might sound contradictory to what I said earlier, but it isn't because YOU are choosing the partner, not your child. Once you're prepared and ready to date, you must look for someone who makes sense for your *entire* life, which includes you, your children, your work, your parents, your siblings, and your friends.

BECOMING A CUSTODIAL DAD: DAVID & AVIGAIL

David and Avigail have been married for ten years. He has two daughters from his first marriage. David's ex-wife, Talia, was a tech exec who traveled frequently for work. Because of Talia's travel schedule, the children began staying with David more and the kids were getting comfortable staying in their dad's space more than their mom's. David was serious about taking his relationship with Avigail to the next level and was ready to propose. David knew he needed someone who was ready to dive into the stepmom role headfirst.

Avigail supported David's plan to become a custodial dad. Talia loved Avigail and considered her to be a great asset to their family dynamic, and Talia knew Avigail would be a great stepmom to her girls and a stand-in when she couldn't be there. Everyone was in agreement. David understood the importance of marrying someone for his entire being.

In addition to picking a person who makes sense for both you and your children, it is important to understand your partner's parenting style. It's great to be attracted to someone and have fun with them, but if you don't see eye to eye on parenting styles, you're roller skating downhill toward the danger zone. When you're seriously dating someone, the parenting style conversation should be high on the list of priority information. What you don't talk about before walking down the aisle will become a bone of contention during your marriage.

One of my favorite things about social media is that it gives people a space to find a community that they relate to and can understand. Sometimes your family and friends can't understand certain dynamics you're experiencing, and that is where finding a community is helpful. Someone reached out to me recently through the @MarryingApParent's Instagram community. A young lady had been watching the page to see if I'd address her issue. She said, "I hate the way my boyfriend parents his son." Her boyfriend's thirteen-year-old son was on the spectrum. She was a special education teacher and in her view, her boyfriend was stifling his son by coddling him. From her professional lens he was high-functioning and self-sufficient, and from her personal interactions with him, she said he was a smart kid with the potential to be an independent adult, but his father and the COBP were holding him back. She said they often argued about his parenting style, and her boyfriend believed she was too harsh to parent his son.

One day after her boyfriend had been working all day, they were in his living room watching a movie together. Her boyfriend was dozing off and his son shouted in the middle of the movie, "I need water!" Like clockwork, her boyfriend began to get up to get the water. She gently put her hand on his leg as he was motioning the recliner chair down and told him, "He can get his own water." Her boyfriend's son looked at her with an annoyed stare and then looked past her and said, "Dad, I'm thirsty. I need water." Her boyfriend began to stand up. "He can get his own water," she said, this time in a more forceful voice. Five seconds felt like five minutes as she watched her boyfriend processing his son's death glare. She said gently, "Sit down, love, he can get his own wat—" and before she could get the word out, his son said loudly, "But I don't want to!" Her boyfriend got up to get the water, and she got up and left the house, furious.

This is a clear picture of a child in full manipulation mode and two people who aren't aligned in parenting. The son was capable, but had gotten so used to his father coddling him that he just didn't want to get up and knew his father would. She said that the two of them [she and her boyfriend] were in love and best friends, but this was the one thing holding her back from marriage and cohabitation. I commended her! It is not easy to yield to caution when we are in love. So often, we look past all the toxins in the name of love.

Parenting is unique. Anyone who has more than one child will tell you that each child is so very different, and what worked for the first child might not work for the last child and most certainly will not work for the middle child (you know how y'all are). Although the children's demeanors might be vastly different, stay aligned with your partner about parenting. When you're dating a parent, you get a front row seat to how that person parents, and if you don't like it, you should talk about it. If it's not something they are willing to change, then they aren't a person you can parent with and thus should no longer date.

When I first began writing this chapter, it was very rigid. I had one school of thought when it came to the order of things: God, spouse, children, and everyone else. Months later, around the time that I had to revise this chapter, it became particularly challenging. What should have taken a few hours took me seven days. During my conversation with Shawn, the pastor from Chicago, I asked, "Even though your wife had this little girl, how did you reconcile with 'the order of things'? I feel like it's God, parents, kids, but some people struggle with that since the kid technically was there before the spouse came along. What are your thoughts?"

I just *knew* he would agree with me, but in true "If you want to make God laugh, tell him about your plans" fashion, he actually did not agree with me at all! He said, "Great question and insight. I knew that I fully trusted God. With that said, everything was in divine order. God knew what I needed to be, which was exactly what he purposed in me. Thus, I couldn't be effective in talking to you if I did not have to instantaneously become a dad. Does that make sense? Romans 8:28 states that all things work together for the good of those who love God and are called to his purpose."

Here is what I've gathered from this insight: If you're a spiritual person and you put God first, everything will be in that order. The order is what it is supposed to be because it came from God. So, even though Pastor Shawn's wife came to him with a daughter, the trust lies in the fact that Pastor Shawn was sent a partner who would understand the importance of the parents being on the same page and in alliance when raising this little girl who predated the marriage, and the little one who would be born of their marriage. Again, even if you aren't a spiritual person, you know that life just *is.* The more present you become, the more you understand that what will be, will be. Being informed and aware will allow you to make better decisions, especially about the order of things. Yours is a custom recipe designed to blend your family together without too much spice.

MAP Title: Establish an order that makes sense for your family.

MAP Legend:

- Establish an order in your home that works for you, your spouse, and your children.
- Learn the characteristics of an enmeshed relationship, and if you are in one, find ways to work through it for a more balanced relationship.
- Do not put unnecessary parenting burdens and responsibilities on your children. Let them be children.
- Your spouse comes before your child and after God.

MAP Directions:

- Do you feel like your children should come before your spouse?
- If your biological children come before your spouse, how do you manage it once you have a child together?
- Does your child get a choice in who you date or marry?

Chapter 5: Stepparenting Is a F*cking Mess

The Brady Bunch was a television series that aired in the sixties, and it was one of the first of its kind to feature a large blended family. It was created by Sherwood Schwartz in 1966, who was inspired after reading that 30% of the marriages in the United States had children from previous relationships. Greg Brady, the father, was a widow. The show never addressed whether Carol Brady, the mom, was divorced or widowed; apparently, at the time, it was considered too risqué to show a divorced woman on television. The sitcom displayed a blended family where the mom had three daughters and the father had three sons, and each episode ended with a lesson in love and family. It was easy and neat, no real mess. Decades later, sitcoms like *Step by Step*, *Moesha*, and *Modern Family* were way more realistic in showing the complex mess that is marrying a parent, stepparenting, and blending families.

"What have I gotten myself into?" That might sound like a really crazy question to ask, but when I realized how difficult it was marrying someone who had a child, I had to process what I had signed up for. When you first start dating someone who has a child, that child (depending on their age) just seems to automatically love you. They pretty much follow along with what they see their parents doing. I think that one of the biggest things that helps the relationship between the new partner and the child is that the child sees that their parent is happy, so it makes them happy too. Children pretty much follow their parent's program, whether it's positive, negative, or neutral. However, children aren't influenced by just one parent, so the simplicity and lightheartedness of the relationship doesn't always last for long, and things can get complicated pretty rapidly.

Oftentimes, the complication begins when the COBP discovers you're around their kid. As we discussed in Chapter 3, I did not have the opportunity to meet the COBP before I met the child. Once the complicating factors entered the relationship, I asked myself, "How long is this journey going to be?" Every time I asked myself this question, it brought up strong emotions that I couldn't identify because they were all firsts for me. It was hard to process what I had gotten myself into because I wasn't prepared for it. And I quickly realized this would be a very long journey without a roadmap.

I had no direction or guidance on what to do with all of the new emotions, confusion, and situations. A few of my friends come from blended families, so I thought seeking their advice would be my best tool. But again, I was wrong. You see, the topics that we address in this book are uncomfortable for people. These are the types of subjects people don't want to be transparent about. They are either embarrassed, like I was, or afraid of people's judgment, like the young lady who contacted me through Instagram.

Honestly, as a stepmom, I found myself trying to just figure it out day by day. I felt alone. Commiserating with other stepparents was helpful sometimes, but there were other times where the things happening in my marriage just seemed dark. The issues with the COBP and my husband appeared to be unique. Not only did I feel isolated, but I felt unsupported by the one person who could have (and perhaps should have) helped me through this very new and daunting process.

Ideally, the parent should be guiding you through this process. But I didn't have that in my marriage, mainly because my ex-husband was still trying to figure it out himself. Needless to say, it was difficult. The earlier years when my stepbaby was younger sometimes felt easier than others, but if I had to truly balance my experience, the hard times definitely outweighed the easier ones. When I look back on it now, I see it did not have to be this hard.

The early days were easier because my stepdaughter was in love with me. I could do no wrong. Although she was being influenced by others around her, she knew my love for her was real and authentic, and at the time she felt the same about me. However, when she turned ten years old things changed, and it was painful. Looking back, the shift made sense. She was older, more aware, and had some big milestones that year. Her age made the people around her more inclined to talk in front of her, which made her mature in a faux way. That false maturity even led me to make what I perceive as the biggest mistake I ever made in our relationship (aside from the immense amount of guilt that I carry for feelings of ABC—abandonment by collateral).

We had a huge picture collage hanging on the wall. I was proud of that collage because I had made it with and in love. There were four large pictures on it. One was a picture of my stepdaughter by herself with a look of pure joy. She was about five years old and I took that picture while I had her suspended in the air on my feet, something that I had done to all of my cousins when we were younger. There was one picture of my son by himself with a soccer ball, wearing a straw vacation hat and a huge smile. Another one was of myself, my stepdaughter, and my ex-husband when we took her on her very first vacation, just the three of us, with my son in my belly. The fourth picture was of my son, my ex-husband, and myself on his very first vacation to Jamaica, just the three of us. My daughter had not been born yet.

One day five years after all of those pictures were taken, as I was braiding my stepdaughter's hair in the kids' playroom, she just happened to look at the picture that had been hanging on the wall for two years. "Munchkin"—that was her name for me—"where is that picture from?" I could still remember it with great clarity. That had been another hard time on the *Marrying ApParent* Richter scale. It was the first in-person interaction that I'd had with the COBP, aside from that day she pulled up next to me in the car, and it was horrible. As if I was in a time machine, sent back to that very moment five years prior, I responded to her question in a cavalier, immature, unprotected manner. I uncharacteristically responded to my very mature bonus daughter, "That was the baby shower we went to that day your mother was talking shit to me."

As the words came out of my mouth, I immediately felt disgusted with myself and watched my "mature" ten-year-old right back into the little four-year-old pre-schooler I'd met six years prior. She continued to ask about it, because it was her experience to have adult conversations, but I stopped. I did not feel right about what was being said. True as it might have been, I pride myself on allowing children to be children, and in six years of horror, I had never ever spoken negatively about the COBP to my stepbaby. It was not my finest moment, and one month later, the conversation reared its ugly head. My stepdaughter shared what I'd said to her mother and finally, after six years of me handling the hardest part of my life as the bigger person, the COBP finally had something to be legitimately pissed about.

After some back and forth, I expressed my thoughts on how she often spoke in front of my stepdaughter about me and my then-husband, and some more back and forth, I stopped myself. "I shouldn't have said that in front of her. I apologized to her [my stepdaughter] as I said it, but let me apologize to you now. It was not my best moment, but it will never happen again." *Silence . . .* "I apologize as well." I let it breathe. Sometimes, you have to just shut up and be wrong, even if it is in the face of someone who has wronged you in the past and would wrong you again in the future. At that moment, it did not matter. I was wrong, and I needed to be accountable for my insensitive words. I never shared information with my stepdaughter again after that. Even when my heart cracked into millions of pieces when I discovered that her parents had an affair, which led to the end of our family unit, I never shared it with her. Just because my heart was broken didn't mean I had to break hers too. If her parents decide to share with her, that's up to them, but unless and until she is an adult, she won't hear it from me. And who knows? Perhaps by the time she is an adult, the urge to protect her will still be there. Whatever it is, however it is shared or not shared, I'd never have negative conversations with her about her parents because she loves them.

You see, you just cannot speak badly about someone a child loves, especially their parent. Once, I went to lunch with a coworker. We were eating and topic hopping like we normally do when he asked me a question that no one had ever asked me, which was, "If you weren't a lawyer, what would you be doing?" My eyes lit up. "Writing a book about marrying a parent," I said. His face was puzzled. The question opened up a dialogue about the *Marrying ApParent* platform and this book. As I explained my purpose project, his face switched from interest to intrigue. My coworker shared that he had been raised in a blended family.

I learned many things about humans while I was interviewing people and writing this book. One of the most profound things that I have noticed is that our inner child is strong and it never really leaves us. As my coworker began to explain his experience, I watched the strong, confident posture of this distinguished gentleman soften into the childlike stature of a young boy:

> My parents got divorced and my dad remarried, and it was rough. My stepmom didn't like my mom, and she talked so badly about her. My mom would have adult conversations

> in front of me and talk negatively about my stepmom. My dad was passive and said nothing. It was hard, and when I look back, it's probably the reason I never had children. What they did scarred me. It went on for decades. One day, my stepmother started talking about my mother and some experience from my childhood and I couldn't take it anymore. At the table in front of the entire family, I looked directly in her eyes and said, "I'm not a kid anymore. You will not talk about my mother ever again," and she never did. I also told my father how his irresponsible silence made room for this battle to go on between my mother and my stepmother.

I have learned my biggest lessons about stepparenting from adult stepchildren. Although my one-off was enough for me to never engage in banter about the COBP ever again, some people don't get the message until it's too late. It doesn't matter how much their parent does or doesn't do for them. It doesn't matter how mature or immature this person is in front of them. You—stepmom, stepdad, and future stepparents in training—cannot and *must not* ever talk badly about the COBP to the child.

I asked my coworker "So, if there was one piece of advice you could give to stepparents, what would it be?" He answered, "Parents and stepparents should have enough love and respect for the children not to have conversations about the other parent in front of them." I nodded in agreement. "This is not just limited to stepparents, either. My mother had no business talking about my stepmom in front of me. It caused preventable negative feelings. In a nutshell: do not talk in front of children."

When I first asked myself the question, "What did I get myself into?" It was a painful open-ended question. This led me to vent to my mother and siblings, who had no experience in what I was going through. They tried to give their best advice. Some of it, I wish I'd have taken heed of; some of it just didn't work with my situation. A few years later, after becoming a wife, a mom, and an official stepmom, I asked myself the question again. It still was foggy, but by being more vulnerable, choosing to open up about my struggles, and talking to other people who were married to or marrying a parent, I realized I wasn't alone, which was comforting. Comfort is great, but it can turn into pure commiseration between hurt people when you have no guidance. We were all blind and trying to provide a sounding board to one another, but we still had no direction or concrete advice.

I was sitting down one day processing why my marriage had differed from those of my parents, my siblings, and my friends who were in "traditional" families, and then it hit me: "Marriage is not as apparent when marrying a parent." It is hella different, and the key difference is that you have to consider a *whole other* adult when making all of your decisions, and plain and simple, it sucks. Once I started interviewing adult stepchildren, the fog cleared a bit more because I could understand how these now healthy adults had processed their biological parents' decisions, like how their biological parent chose to bring their stepparent into their life. And finally, eight years later, I asked myself again, "What did I get myself into?" and with crystal-clear clarity, I could finally answer it: a f*cking mess!

When you think about it, mess—"a dirty or untidy place or situation"—is temporary. Some people take their shoes off as soon as they enter their homes. Although I did not grow up doing this, between visiting other people's homes over the years that do—and dodging poop living in Hell's Kitchen, NYC, where I swear there are more dogs than people—I have adopted the custom and now take my shoes off as soon as I enter my home. When I first started this practice, because it was unfamiliar to me, I watched one pair of shoes turn into sixty-five shoes in my entryway. No, not sixty-six, but sixty-five, because my daughter always loses a shoe or three, so the pairs are often left lonely. I'm a minimalist, and the mess in my entryway was enough to send me over a cliff . . . but mess is temporary. As I stared at the mess, I decided I had to come up with a solution: a shoe rack! Simple. A shoe rack was at every entryway when we lived in my house on Long Island, and there is a shoe rack in the closet in my apartment now. A shoe rack was the permanent fix to my temporary mess.

Stepparenting is a mess, but the mess is temporary. Yes, in some cases it will last for years, but it's still just temporary. So, how do you fix the stepparenting mess? What tool can you pull from Mickey's Mouseketools or Dora's *mochilla* (backpack)? I had a revelation: marrying a parent and stepparenting are filled with unconditional love. "How cliche!" is what you're thinking, right? It's not, though.

Unconditional love is an interesting phrase because love, as it is defined in both dictionaries and religious texts, has no conditions. Love, the verb, means "to hold dear; to cherish." "Cherish" means to keep or cultivate with care and affection. The prefix "–un" when added to verbs means the reversal or cancellation of an action or state, denoting deprivation, separation, or reduction to a lesser state. "Unconditional" means there is no influence or determination into the thing; it just is. "Unconditional" means not subject to any conditions. Simple. "Condition"—as a verb, means having a significant influence or to bring something into the desired state of use. By definition, the prefix "–un" is only added to verbs and adjectives. Love is a noun but also a powerful verb because it requires action. Unconditional love allowed me to plan parties for my bonus daughter, stay up late and do last-minute projects with her, do her hair in beautiful styles, pull over on the side of the road when she was crying, change her clothes and bed sheets in the middle of the night when she threw up, all of it. It was all action, all doing, all cultivation with care and affection. It's love.

Stepparenting—loving a child that you did not birth, a child you did not choose, a child who, but for the parent you fell in love with, would never otherwise be in your life—is pure unconditional love. In my humble opinion, there is nothing more unconditional than loving someone else's child. The condition, the parent, is *how* you have come to know your stepchild, but the love you have for them is boundless. There are no intertwined strings of DNA that tie you to that child. There is no legal obligation that ties you to them, either; it's only love that links you, and that is beautiful. The love that I have for my stepdaughter is still there. It's why I feel so connected to her, even though I don't see her. It's why I miss her so much. It's why you *don't throw the baby out with the bathwater.* Marrying a parent, it's unconditional love. It's taking on someone's child, their responsibilities to that child, the basic necessities, the raising and rearing, and stepping in when a COBP is not around, either physically or mentally.

Marrying a parent is a beautiful *temporarily* difficult journey that *can* be more apparent with knowledge, a roadmap, communication, boundaries, and pure, unconditional, unadulterated love for the parent, the child, and perhaps one day, with a heap of healing and maybe just because you love the child, the COBP. Although I truly believe in unconditional love, I also believe in love and respect of self. There is no human or situation that should cause you to continuously feel disrespected or unloved.

MAP Title: Clean the mess with unconditional love.

MAP Legend:

- Sometimes stepparenting feels like a mess!
- It's okay to be transparent about your stepparenting journey.
- Unconditional love doesn't mean you have to accept disrespect.

MAP Directions:

- Who do you talk to regarding the complexities of your relationship with the COBP?
- What types of situations are recurring in your relationship with the COBP?
- How can you facilitate a future where your partner and COBP can peacefully coexist?

Chapter 6: Invitation Only

Marriage is the union of two people as partners. Partners are a pair of people engaged together in the same activity. In short, whatever your spouse is doing, you should be doing. Whether that manifests in being physically present or supporting one another mentally, emotionally, and spiritually, you should be of one accord when it comes to the activities you're involved in. Allowing any thing, any person, or any event to physically or psychologically divide you and your spouse is the beginning of the breakdown of your union. In Chapter 4, The Order of Things, we talked about the family system and the boundaries between members of the family. In essence, your children should stand beside you and your spouse, never *between* you and your spouse. In theory, if you have become one—meaning you're successfully partnered and paired—the oneness of this new entity means that nothing can come in between it. Because of the child's inherent link to the COBP, to allow your children to come between you and your partner also allows the COBP to be in the middle of your union, thus splitting the family.

Parents, as you consider marriage, one of the action items you should implement is learning how to protect your partner from anything outside of the union. Learn how to guard them from all attempts to disrupt their peace. This includes work, vices, and habits, and the most challenging disruptor, people. It's not the strangers you need to worry about—that will be easy! It's the friends and family who will test you and whether you're ready to be in that union. You will face the most opposition from your parents, siblings, and children, along with all of the things, events, and people connected to them, including the COBP.

Singles, one of the greatest challenges of marrying a parent is that there is another adult who is not part of your family who can greatly affect your partner's decisions, emotions, and mood. A parent who is ready to date or is protecting their marriage will ensure that the things affected by the COBP don't have a negative impact on their spouse and their children. The single who is ready to marry a parent will also be supportive and hold space for their spouse and the ups and downs that will inevitably occur.

Braxton Family Values was a reality show on the We TV network. The show starred the Braxton sisters: Toni, Tamar, Trina, Traci, and Towanda, plus their mom, Evelyn. There were special appearances from their brother, Mikey, and father, Michael Braxton Sr. At some point Michael Braxton Sr. had gotten remarried, and the marriage seemed to be a sore spot for the Braxton sisters. In one of the early episodes, Trina Braxton begins to open up about her relationship with her father. Trina originally married her then-husband, the late Gabe Solis, in 2003. In an episode from season two, the entire family was in St. Lucia attending Toni's show, and Trina decided to renew her vows with Gabe. During her confessional interview segment, we learn that Trina's father did not attend his daughter's wedding. "My dad was not at my original wedding date because I didn't invite his wife, so he had chosen not to come," Trina revealed. "Every girl wants her dad to walk her down the aisle. To finally have that moment was a dream come true." From this short segment, it appeared Trina's stepmother was the reason that Trina's father did not attend the wedding. However, later we learn something to the contrary.

The Braxton sisters, their mom, and their father traveled to Mexico for a family vacation in season five. Unbeknownst to his daughters and his ex-wife, Mr. Braxton brought his wife on the trip. His wife was still a sore spot for the sisters and his ex-wife. In the episode, we discover that Michael Sr. was involved with his current wife, Wanda, while he was still married to his former bride, Evelyn. It's evident in the episode that they are respectful to Wanda, but out of loyalty to their mom, they don't invite their stepmother to events. When their mother finds out that her ex-husband is in Mexico with his wife, she leaves and heads back to the United States. Once she leaves, Toni decides to invite her father and his wife to dinner to finally have a discussion and clear the air.

First, they bring up Trina's first wedding. Remember how in season two we were led to believe that her father did not walk her down the aisle at her first wedding because his wife wasn't invited and did not want him to attend either? Well, Mr. Braxton begins to explain that this was the second child who had not invited his wife to their wedding. The first time, with Toni, he attended, but he said the second time, he was done with the ultimatums and chose not to go. He continued to say that in both instances, Wanda told him to go celebrate with his children and walk them down the aisle, but it was his decision not to go.

Even as adult women, it was clear that it was hard for the Braxton sisters to accept their father's wife who was once his mistress, especially because their mother was still angry about it. Even though he had been married to his current wife for over fifteen years, in the words of Tamar, "You can't put time on hurt." If you have married a parent and you're part of the reason the marriage ended, you have to understand the hurt feelings. Although the union itself had been questionable to those involved, Wanda did the right thing by encouraging her husband to attend his daughter's wedding. Plus, she earned cool points in my book by not pushing for a spot on the guest list. Michael should have honored his daughter and respected his wife's encouragement. If you married or were a mistress or manstress (I just made that word up, because women make poor choices too) and get invited to such a significant family event, then you need to show grace, because this event ain't about you.

In all other instances, the stepparent should be at the child's events, and NO ONE should prevent them from being there. By no means should the COBP have any say in whether the stepparent is allowed to attend any events. Holding space for your partner means understanding the scenarios that they might incur and fully supporting them. As a stepparent, this might mean encouraging your spouse to attend an event that you may not have been invited to yourself. As the parent, you have to know when to make the tough choices, and if you pick a supportive partner, you will make the right choice majority of the time. It is the nature of a parent to protect their child. Control, however, is not the same as protection. When there is a celebration or event for a child, it is a very controlling move on the part of any parent to exclude any of the child's loved ones, including their stepparent—especially a stepparent who is helping to raise the child! The stepparent should be invited to every event that the parent is invited to.

THE CREATIVE STEPMOM: JENNIFER

Over the years, I have had the pleasure of chatting with some pretty amazing stepparents. One of the stepmoms, Jennifer, is a friend from high school. She has always had a great sense of humor and is a strong human. What I love most about how she stepparents is that "step–" just doesn't exist in her vocabulary. Jennifer refers to her husband's biological children as her daughters—not bonus babies, not stepdaughters, simply "my daughters." Jennifer is a funny person by nature, but she is no joke. One of her daughters was graduating from junior high school right after COVID, so although the graduation was outside, the school limited the number of tickets that each student would receive to two. In a situation like this, there wouldn't be much of a discussion. Both the father, Jennifer's husband, and the COBP were fully involved in their daughter's lives, so naturally, one ticket would go to her father and the other to her mother.

Jennifer could have taken this moment and made it about her feelings. She could have stayed home, pouted, talked to her friends, and been angry. But the graduation was outside and could be seen and heard from the other side of the gates, so Jennifer dressed up and recorded the entire ceremony through the holes in the metal fence. When her bonus baby's name was called, she screamed for her as if she was up front in one of the ticketed seats.

Lack of a ticket did not stop Jennifer from showing up for her oldest daughter! Jennifer's actions showed love, happiness, and if nothing else, it showed that she was a parent too. On the occasions that your stepchild gets only two tickets to their event, then you'll have to sit that one out, but you should be right at that restaurant afterwards eating spinach dip and cake and celebrating with your stepbaby, spouse, and everyone else.

MAP Title: Stepparents should attend all special events that parents attend.

MAP Legend:

- You should never be okay going somewhere where your spouse wasn't invited.
- If you're married to a parent who would attend events without you, you need to go to therapy immediately and reset some boundaries.

MAP Directions:

- Are there any instances where you would be okay attending your child's events without your spouse?
- Does your child or COBP play a role in setting the tone in your relationships?
- How can your partner best support you in instances where your child or the COBP doesn't want them around?

Chapter 7: Rules & Roles

Learning the rules of a household takes skill. Growing up in a two-parent household meant learning how both my mom and my dad operated. That meant knowing which parent to ask, "Can I go down the block to Christine's house and watch SNICK?" and even more, it meant knowing that the response could vary per parent at any given time. Looking back, being a child took wisdom. Wisdom was knowing that my dad worked nights, and a tired Daddy would say yes to most things right before falling off into a nap before work. Learning my father, however, meant knowing that the response would be vastly different once he awakened from that nap prematurely and had to head to work. With my mom, wisdom meant knowing that if all of the Saturday chores were done without me having to be told, SNICK wasn't even a question—it was going down. Understanding the household rules and navigating adults as a minor takes skill, endurance, and if you're lucky, an older sibling or two who have known your parents way longer than you.

When you marry a parent, figuring out the household roles and rules is even more of a mission. You come into a marriage and, for the most part, probably parent the same way you were parented. Now mix in your experience and combine it with your spouse's and the COBP's parenting styles—oh, and add in a pinch of the manipulative nature of a child who is figuring out how to be part of a blended family—and you have a very spicy sauce! A sauce so spicy, you can lose your voice. So many stepparents lose their voice in their marriages.

Sarah Jakes Roberts and Touré Roberts serve as co-pastors of The Potter's House in Dallas and Los Angeles. They are a blended family with a total of six children. Sarah came into the marriage with two biological children, Touré came with three, and they share one together. Jakes Roberts explains in her *NY Times* best-selling book, *Power Moves*, that when she and her husband initially started merging their family, she felt uncertain about asking her bonus children to help with the housework.[13] Sarah goes on to explain that when her husband pushed her to hold the kids accountable to her values, she resisted his advice and continued playing the role as the "cool parent," requiring her to do twice as much work to care for a large family. She went from being a single mom of two to a married mom caring for a family of eight. It wasn't until she reached her breaking point that she was able to take her husband's advice and find her voice.

Touré embodies the concept of "your spouse is your teammate." He could have stayed silent or allowed his wife to continue "doing too much." Some parents have a difficult time having their partner's back over their children's, but instead, he encouraged her to take a stance. I don't know if he realized this at the time, but when Tourè Roberts urged his wife, "hold them accountable," he created a trust in their marriage. Through these

---

[13] Sarah Jakes Roberts, *Power Moves* (W Publishing Group, 2024).

words, he established her role as the mother in that house and gave her the freedom to mother his children the way she mothered her own. He gave her a voice—something that many stepparents lose or feel like they don't have when parenting their stepchildren —and he had his wife's back, which in my opinion is the most important tenet in a marriage.

For the parent, it's your job to facilitate the relationships between your spouse and your child and, if necessary, the COBP. You and your spouse must see eye to eye on parenting. If you don't, you're in for a rude awakening. This is a premarital conversation that you *must* have. The rules and roles of your household need to be clearly communicated, and most of all, you and your spouse must be on the same page when it comes to those rules.

A SPECIAL BLEND

Stacy grew up in a blended family and recalled a childhood story featuring a family dinner at her father's house. "We were eating and I asked for something to drink. My stepmom told me no. I said, in the most bratty and rude tone, 'But I'm thirsty!' My stepmom responded, 'You can have something to drink after you finish dinner.' Like I had no damn sense, and with my father's piercing stare looking at me from across the table, I doubled down and responded, 'Well my *mom* lets me drink juice while I eat dinner.'" Now at this very moment, every parent—whether you're biologically a parent or a parent by marriage—knows where this could have gone. Poor Stacy was setting herself up for trouble. At any moment, a shoe was about to fly across that table! Stacy continued, "I knew this could go left.

My father did not stand for disrespect, and this was the first time I had ever challenged any adult in my life. My stepmom took a deep breath and calmly responded, 'When you're with your mom, you can drink during dinner. When you're here, our rules are that you drink after dinner.' Her calm tone eased the thick tension in the air, and it was at the moment that I learned that their rules were different, and I had to get used to that."

Stacy's stepmom set the stage early on about the rules and the roles. With her gentle but firm stance, she let Stacy know that there were rules in their home and that she had an authority role in the home. At the very first moment that Stacy tried her, Stacy's stepmother used her voice. This isn't always the case for stepparents, because when the parent doesn't properly set the stage and/or doesn't support the stepparent, you will find yourself trying to appease your stepchild and playing a role that is unsustainable as a parent. Trying to be your stepchild's friend, to be the "cool parent," and constantly trying to get your spouse to be on your side when stepparenting is an unsustainable, exhausting experience. In *Power Moves*, Sarah Jakes Roberts poignantly describes the type of relationship that can only survive if you're constantly overexerting yourself as comparable to being held hostage. Under the circumstances, it is impossible to experience true freedom.[14] Stacy's father did not have to say a word, but his actions showed that he fully supported his wife, which allowed her the freedom to be authentic herself. Marrying a parent is a team effort, and your spouse is your teammate.

---

[14] *Ibid.*

To a child, anything that differs from what goes on in their custodial setting is going to buck the system. So, in order for the bucking to be minimal, there has to be consistency, and that means that the parent and the bonus parent must be united. Any inkling that there is a glitch in the matrix and like a mouse through a pinhole, contention will weasel into your marriage and the "evil stepparent" will be born. The problem with contention in a blended family is that it will never be blamed on the biological parent.

According to Dr. Sheryl Ziegler, generally, fathers tend to struggle more with setting rules, possibly because this wasn't their role in the previous marriage. Now, they find themselves filling both parental roles, which can be overwhelming. Fathers often experience more guilt due to the stress of divorce, and with a new marriage and additional children, this guilt can lead to inconsistent enforcement of rules.[15] There is inherent guilt and a looming "Did I do the right thing?" that flows in and out of your mind after divorce, separation, or even just coming to grips with knowing that you and the person you had a child with will never be together. You feel regret because you assume that the best situation for your child is for you and their other biological parent to be together as a nuclear family. So, instead of being honest with yourself and accepting that perhaps the nuclear family was *not* the best situation, you fantasize about what could have been and allow your own

---

[15] Sheryl Ziegler, "The Only Marriage Advice For Blended Families You'll Ever Need," *Medium*, October 10, 2017, https://medium.com/@DrSherylZiegler/the-only-marriage-advice-for-blended-families-youll-ever-need-c29ffa65ead4.

imagination to manipulate you. That guilt, if not dealt with, goes along with you in the baggage you carry into the new relationship, and when you open your bags to unpack, the stench of the guilt hops from you to your partner.

Touré Roberts wouldn't have been able to tell his wife to hold the children accountable to the standards that she valued if he came into the marriage parenting from a space of guilt. Perhaps instead, he may have said something like, "I don't want to bother them and have them do chores. They are only here three times a week." Sarah would have still inevitably reached her breaking point, and when she did—and perhaps blew up and screamed at everyone—without the support of her spouse, she would have ended up looking like the unstable parent who can't control her anger. If Stacy's father would have given her the juice, he would have undermined the rules they established in their household, showed his daughter that it was okay for her to be disrespectful, and potentially caused an argument between himself and his wife. It appears that both Stacy's dad and Touré came into their new marriages without the guilt in their luggage. I'm sure that they had their moments of feeling remorseful for their children, but the support they had for their spouses displayed that those moments were fleeting and did not hold enough space for their marriage to suffer for it.

You can imagine kids saying things like, "Why do we always have to do chores when we come over here?" or labeling their stepparent as a "mean person" all because of some unaddressed guilt from their parent. If the kids witnessed their parent not holding them accountable and not supporting their stepparent, then the biological parent would get to play the "cool parent" role, while the stepparent would end up looking like a hothead. Kids rarely blame their biological parent when things go wrong, and it is unfair to set your partner up for that type of failure.

Ziegler suggests that you should consider your common set of values as the cornerstone for establishing your household rules.[16] Establish rules that work for your family and stand firm with those rules. As parents and stepparents, you have to be strong enough to talk to each other about tweaking the rules as they get older or as seasons change. You may not always agree on the changes, but it's okay to be flexible when there is a rule change that makes sense for the family. No matter what, however, your front must remain united in front of the kids when establishing the rules and roles of the household.

MAP Title: The rules that apply are where you rest your head that night.

MAP Legend:

- You may not be on the same page as your COBP when it comes to rules, but you and your spouse should be on the same page.
- Feeling guilty or remorseful is normal after a breakup, but don't let it control how you parent your children.
- Support your partner's rule as the stepparent and the mother or father figure in the home.

---

[16] *Ibid.*

MAP Directions:

- Do you have feelings of remorse because you and your COBP are no longer together?
- What role do you want your partner to play with your child?
- What would you do if your child was disrespectful to their stepparent?

Chapter 8: When the Weapon Formed Is Your Child

Imagine your favorite little human becoming someone you begin to despise. Not because they crashed your car or because they lied to the teacher and you had to go up to the school, but because the little being who has your eyes and disposition is being coached, coaxed, and brainwashed by their other biological parent to dislike you or their stepparent. The indoctrination of the child to hate you and your new wife, husband, or partner turns the child into a dagger, and boy, what a rusty rigid dagger they become. That weapon—your precious baby—thrusts, jabs, lunges, and twists into your back with each visit. And like any victim of violence, the site of the weapon begins to trigger massive defense mechanisms, and ultimately you go into protective mode over your own emotions.

The weaponizing of a child is pure evil, but it's done so very often. It could be minute but oftentimes it is a grand display, and the child, depending on their age and maturity level, cannot decipher what is happening or realize that their own parent who is supposed to love them is, in fact, using them. When the child is a bit more mature, the other biological parent may have a hard time weaponizing the child against their own parent, and that's where the bonus parent becomes the victim of the affliction.

CUSTODY BATTLE: BREANNE & SAM

Breanne and Sam share seven-year-old twins. They have an extremely tumultuous relationship and have been in a custody battle since the twins were four months old. Sam and his fiancée of four years recently had a small wedding. Sam and his fiancée strategically decided to plan the wedding on a day that they would have the twins, as they did not want to run the risk of Breanne stopping the girls from coming to their wedding. Sam is a family-oriented man; he was raising his daughters with his fiancée and wanted to make sure his girls were part of his special day. The twins were excited to be flower girls at their dad and stepmom's wedding. They bought the girls beautiful dresses, and they were elated to be able to get their hair and a little bit of makeup done for the wedding. Sam and his fiancée decided that they wouldn't share their news with Breanne because she had a history of causing major issues on special days. After their beautiful wedding day, Sam dropped the girls off with Breanne for their weekend visit.

When the twins got back home to Sam on Sunday, their behavior was off, and they were being extremely rude to their father and stepmom. They would barely speak to him, rolled their eyes when he spoke, and mumbled under their breath when their stepmom asked questions. Breanne called them on FaceTime a few hours after they were home, and Sam could hear Breanne having a very mature and inappropriate conversation with the twins about Sam. Sam walked into the room and took the twins' iPad. He attempted to have a conversation with Breanne, but it went left as it had many times before. Sam went back to the girls' bedroom to talk to them and one of the twins said, "Mommy said you're a liar." The other one followed up, "You lied to us." Sam was confused. As his wife came into the room, the twins looked away and got quiet. Sam asked, "What is going on?" One of his daughters replied, "You didn't tell our mom that you were getting married. You're a liar, Dad."

Sam took a deep breath. He had to reset and decide how he was going to handle this. His first instinct was to be angry and yell. "How dare these children speak to me like this," he thought. "I would have never called my parents liars. They would have *slapped me into next Tuesday!*" After a moment, Sam decided that he would have to have an uncomfortable conversation with his daughters. He gently explained that it was very important for them to be at the wedding and that sometimes Mom had a hard time with decisions that Dad made. "I did not lie to your mom or you girls," he said, "but I understand why you have these big feelings. I'm sorry if anything that I did or said to you has hurt you." The girls began to cry, and then they talked for a while. He allowed his daughters to ask any questions that were plaguing them. There were moments of anger, sadness, and confusion, but Sam did his best to have the conversation with his daughters with understanding and love.

Fortunately, in Sam's home, the weaponizing didn't last past that moment. But in many households, especially in families where the weaponizing is being done by the custodial parent, this kind of behavior can have permanent effects. Using your child against their other parent is diabolical. An article in *Psychology Today* discusses child weaponization, also known as parental alienation, where one parent intentionally manipulates the child to turn them against the other parent.[17] Little can be more painful than for a mother or father to experience this hugely destructive process. A positive bond that may have existed for years can be severed in a matter of seconds by a parent who maliciously and successfully mounts a campaign of constant denigration against the other.

Parental alienation can be incredibly distressing for a child, leading to feelings of confusion, sadness, and loneliness due to the loss. A child might struggle to understand why they still love one parent when the other expresses such intense dislike. Without any proof to challenge the falsehoods told by one parent, the child is left in emotional turmoil. Moreover, they are unable to properly grieve the estranged relationship because the separation feels uncertain and may change over time.[18] Some children become convinced that not only are they better off with just one parent, but also that the other is toxic. Some are just confused as to why the people who made them have negative feelings toward one another. Another frequent outcome is that the child may start to refuse to spend time with or even to speak with the alienated parent.

Paying attention to how a parent speaks about their COBP is crucial when dating. Venting about a current issue that is bothersome is okay. However, if

---

17 "Parental Alienation," Psychology Today, accessed June 3, 2024, https://www.psychologytoday.com/us/basics/parental-alienation.

18 *Ibid.*

you find the parent lingering on old topics or constantly and consistently bad-mouthing the COBP, you may be dealing with someone who has not yet been able to recover from the breakdown of the relationship. Allow me a moment of candor: It takes strength, endurance, and love for your children to not weaponize them. For me, it's never been a thought to weaponize my children against their dad, and that's because I love them too much to do so. I have had friends who are both custodial and noncustodial parents, both men and women who have either been the victim or the perpetrator of child weaponization or parental alienation. And their situations taught me that weaponizing your children affects not just the other parent; it is also really troublesome and damaging to the children.

If you have been the victim of this type of parental alienation or the COBP using your child as a pawn, it's important that you seek professional help from a family lawyer and a family therapist. If you're the parent using your child as a pawn, having inappropriate conversations with your child about their other parent, or you're still in pain because of the end of the relationship, try your hardest to stop. I get that there may be pain connected to your COBP. I understand that you might be angry because they aren't helping financially or physically. You probably have so much on your plate, and honestly you have the right to be angry if this is your situation, but think about your child first. If it is an emotional response, seek some help from a therapist and heal the wounds that are causing you to be upset. If it is a response from the lack of help, reach out to a lawyer so you can get the help you need. Whatever you choose to do, know that you have power, and you can prevent the infliction of more pain on your child.

MAP Title: Don't use your child as a weapon to hurt their other parent, because it hurts the child too.

MAP Legend:
Parents:

- Your child is not your therapist. Do not use them to help you manage your relationship with their other parent.
- Seek family therapy to deal with challenges with your COBP.

Singles:

- Pay attention to how your partner speaks about their COBP in front of their child.

MAP Directions:

- What kinds of discussions do you have with your child about your COBP?
- Has your COBP ever stopped you from seeing your child?
- In what circumstances would you prevent your COBP from seeing your child?
- How do you ensure that your child's best interests are prioritized in your interactions with your COBP?

Chapter 9: Know When to Go!

There were a few times throughout my last year of the marriage where the signs were telling me that it was time to go. The deal-breakers had been broken, and my spirit was having trouble bearing the weight from our cracked foundation. The glaring signs weren't easy to ignore, but to be honest, there were two things that allowed me to ignore the signs and hold back from leaving the marriage: my children and this book. Plus, making the decision to end my marriage was challenging, sad, and scary.

We become so attached to our experiences that the fear of anything new keeps us trapped in a holding pattern. For me, it was the "nuclear" family. Families are made up of imperfect people, so there is nothing about anyone's family (I don't care *how* many cute pictures and videos they post) that is perfect. Growing up, my nuclear family wasn't perfect, but something about being in the same household as both parents was normal. It was a very special, loving, fun norm, but my norm.

My children's experience was supposed to be as close to my norm as possible: mom and dad in the same house together, married until one of us died. We were already part of a blended family, but for my biological children, they were to have the closest experience to a nuclear family as possible. I wanted my children to grow up like me, in a two-parent household. Leaving the marriage meant facing the ugly truth that I would be a solo parent, the devastating truth that I'd wake up some mornings without my children in the same home as me, the anxious truth that my children might be raised and influenced by a stepmother that I did not get along with, and the difficult truth that I had to detach from "my norm."

The other concern I had, oddly enough, was this book. My publishing dream kept me in an unhealthy marriage because I felt like this is one of my babies too. This book was born because of my experiences and when I considered stepping away, I had to consider one burning question: How could I publish about *Marrying ApParent* when I was on the road to *divorcing* a parent?

In my whimsical mind, I would hurry up and get the book published and then move forward with getting out of the marriage. Well, God had other plans for me. God wanted me out of my marriage, and I can say this with conviction because God is the one who gave me clear signs—and I mean CLEAR! I don't mean a slight wind blowing when I asked for a sign, or a leaf gently landing on my knee. He sent a brick to my face.

On an episode of *The Jamie Kern Lima Show* entitled "Oprah's Life-Changing Lessons: Hear Your Intuition, Find Purpose & Live Your Best Life Now!" Lima prompted Oprah to recount her metaphor about the whisper, the brick, and the wall collapsing. Oprah explained that when first God communicates, it starts as a mere whisper. If you fail to heed that, a metaphorical brick will hit you, signaling a problem. Ignoring the brick leads to a tsunami, which signifies a complete disaster.[19] For many of us, the whisper is that first response that goes across your mind when you're faced with a question. It's an instinct, the primal response before thought enters and before you can call your parent, sibling, best friend, or therapist. *That's* the whisper. It's hard to lean into the whisper because we have so many loud noises, both internally and externally, that have the ability to drown out our own voices.

God has always spoken to me two ways: through my gut and through my dreams. I had never considered "the whisper, the brick, and the tsunami," but now that I can associate my experience with words, I can clearly understand the metaphor. My initial feelings after a dealbreaker were my whispers. For me, the feeling always sits right in the pit of my stomach. It is a physical manifestation of the whisper. My stomach would actually start burning. Again, internal and external noise will mute your whisper to silence. An external source might tell you you're paranoid for expressing what the whisper is saying to you. An internal force might let fear silence it. When I ignored the fire in my stomach, God would send a vivid dream—my brick.

Exactly one month (to the day!) before I found out about the affair, I had a vivid dream that I was shopping in the mall with my husband. In one of the windows, like a mannequin, stood my husband's ex . . . naked. He was standing there, staring at her. I remember watching him watching her and waking up

---

19 Jamie Kern Lima, "Oprah Reveals All: Life-Changing Lessons on Weight, Shame and Worthiness! (pt 1)," *YouTube*, Posted June 25, 2024, [add runtime of video, like 1:10:03 for an hour, 10 minutes, and 3 seconds], https://www.youtube.com/watch?v=Jo6dGt3Pysk.

feeling sick. I immediately sat up and texted my sister. I remember the date because I still have the text in my phone. Dreams like this go directly in my notes or in a text to a loved one so that I can recall it the next day and go look it up on a dream interpretation website. I began to have vivid dreams at eighteen years old. Years later, when my father passed, I began to record the dreams in my notepad because I would forget the details once I woke up the next morning.

When I woke up, I researched the dream and read that dreaming about your partner's ex-girlfriend indicates your own insecurities. It suggests that you might sense she still has some presence in your relationship, whether on a physical or psychological level.[20] This hit deep, because you could have never convinced me that they had a physical relationship. I was wrong, and the whisper had been telling me for months. When the tsunami hit and I had proof that it was true, I had to leave. There was no turning back. This was just one of those deal-breakers that couldn't be repaired.

So now, not only did I have to break up with the ideals of having my family all under one roof—I had to leave behind this book, too. Right? WRONG! First God said, "You didn't title it *Marrying ApParent* for no reason." One of the definitions for the word "apparent," according to the Cambridge Dictionary, is "able to be seen or understood." "Marriage is not as apparent when marrying a parent" was the tagline that birthed the title and brand *Marrying ApParent.* That extra *P* could stand

[20] "Dream Moods Dream Themes: Relationships," *Dream Moods,* accessed March 10, 2023, https://www.dreammoods.com/dreamthemes/relationships-dream-symbols.htm.

for so many things—problems, pulchritudinous, perimeters, and perspective, just to name a few. The type of marriages that I witnessed growing up, the marriages that we often modeled our own after, didn't include additional parents or progeny, so *nothing* about this journey of marrying a parent was actually apparent. Instead it was obscure, uncertain, and taboo.

On an episode of Super Soul Sunday that airs on OWN (the Oprah Winfrey Network) Pastor John Gray explained that when you develop a deeper understanding of someone else's pain, God is broadening your perspective.[21] It hit me like a ton of bricks—I was about to be launched into a new stratosphere. This story of help had not been ripe when I was a single girl dating a parent. It hadn't been ready when I became a stepmom. This book couldn't have been written until I became a solo parent, and only then could I give a true experience of what could have helped Single Erica, Stepmom Erica, and Solo Mom Erica. So, now I get to teach the community about marrying a parent from three different perspectives. All of this means that I get to leave the tears on these pages. I get to heal, you get to heal, *we* get to heal. Singles dating parents get to become more aware. Stepparents get the opportunity to use these conversation starters to recalibrate their marriages and learn to have a voice and no longer be silenced, and also to listen and learn from their spouse. Lastly, parents learn how to date, set boundaries with their COBP, be loving listeners to their future partners, and set the stage

[21] OWN, "Oprah Speaks with Pastor John Gray About Purpose," *YouTube,* Posted April 17, 2017, [add runtime of video], https://www.youtube.com/watch?v=l9SC-U58Yk8.

for a healthy marriage and a blended family (if they so choose).

The current estimated divorce rate for stepfamily couples is approximately 45-50%, with a projected rate of about 50-60%.[22] Divorce is particularly hard. Often, one person feels forced to make this decision because a specific circumstance or set of circumstances have affected the marriage. In an article titled "The link between stepkids and divorce—and how you can beat the odds," Gail Rosenblum writes that if marriage is hard, and marriage with our own kids is harder, then marriage in a blended clan is often the most challenging with all it brings, including unresolved drama with exes, financial stress, differing parenting styles, and questionable loyalties that can take on even greater intensity in the blended family. Although stepchildren are one of the causes of divorce in blended families, that certainly was not my situation. As a matter of fact, my bonus baby was a huge reason why I stayed too. I had been in her life since she was four years old, and she was as much a norm to me as my biological children. But the circumstances surrounding what occurred were too devastating, so after careful consideration, I decided that I needed to file for divorce.

Knowing when to go is not only for married people; it's for singles and parents as well. Reality shows have made relationships part of our viewing pleasure, especially ones focused on marriage. *Put a Ring on It* (on OWN) was described as a social experiment for long-time couples to discover if they're truly meant to be.

---

[22] Ron L. Deal, "*The Smart Stepfamily: Seven Steps to a Healthy Family,*" 2016, christianaudio.com.

Here's the thing—one of them is ready for marriage and the other is on the fence, so they both are encouraged to date other people to see if it's time to get married or start a new relationship with someone else. Rarely do dating shows highlight or showcase parents, so I was quite fascinated by one couple's story in season one of the show. The boyfriend, Michael, was a dad in a relationship with Che. Michael made it clear to Che that he wasn't ready for marriage. Years prior, Michael and his COBP had agreed that their son would move in with his dad when he started high school.

Che was ready to do the slow strut to the altar, but she wasn't amenable to Michael's son moving in with them. According to Michael, adding his son into his daily life with Che was a huge hurdle. But if they could jump over this "hurdle" together, he'd be more likely to propose. In the confessional scene, Che dropped a major truth bomb: she didn't want Michael's kid living with them.

Analyzing this from both sides, there's a red flag on the field for the single *and* the parent. Let's talk about Che first. Her statements were the most alarming. Her words could easily be seen as a red flag, but were they? Looking at it objectively, she was dating a noncustodial father whose son lived in a totally different state. Perhaps she had become accustomed to it being just the two of them and Michael never required her to get comfortable with custodial fatherhood. Here's the problem: Che was okay with Michael being a show parent. I'd say Che's "know when to go" moment was when she realized that her boyfriend was not a co-parent to his child's mom.

As for Michael, his "know when to go" moment was when Che explicitly said that she did not want a kid living in her home. Michael had agreed to take his son long before Che entered the picture. His plans should have been with Che early on, and especially before they moved in together. Instead, they continued to date. They shouldn't have passed "go" if Michael's son moving in was not an option for Che. She shouldn't have even been Michael's girlfriend! She had every right not to want kids, but when you date someone who is a parent, you're deciding that you don't mind being a parent (at some point). If that doesn't sit well with you, and IT'S OKAY IF IT DOESN'T, then you shouldn't date a parent. As the parent, Michael should've realized that Che wasn't long-term partner material. If she could not make space in her heart and home for Michael's son, how could he fully show up in all of his roles, especially as a father?

MAP Title: Listen to the whispers and know that it is okay to walk away.

MAP Legend:

- A person you're dating who doesn't embrace your child is a person you should walk away from.
- A person who is okay not being a full parent is your "know when to go" flag.
- If you aren't ready to be a parent, don't date a parent.

MAP Directions:

- When did you know that it was time to walk away from your COBP?
- What types of actions or behaviors would cause you to choose yourself over the family unit?

Chapter 10: Don't Throw the Baby Out with the Bathwater

About two months after my marital reality was shattered with news of the affair, I fled to the beach. It's one of my safe spaces. I'd have done it sooner, but I had a brand-new job and hadn't accrued any paid time off yet. It was Memorial Day Weekend and I took a last-minute flight to the W Hotel in Fort Lauderdale, my favorite place to decompress. While on the flight, I watched the movie *Clueless*. Cher, the main character played by actress Alicia Silverstone, was a rich teenager from Beverly Hills and the only child to her late mother (not featured in the film) and father, Mel Horowitz, a high-powered attorney played by actor Dan Hedaya. Years after the death of his wife, when Cher was already a teenager, Mel Horowitz briefly married Gail Lucas (also not featured in the movie) who had a son, Josh Lucas, played by Paul Rudd. One morning at breakfast, a conversation similar to this takes place between Cher and her litigator father:

Mr. Horowitz: Josh is in town and will be joining us for dinner.
Cher: For what? [She's frustrated by this news.]
Mr. Horowitz: He's my stepson.

Cher: You were barely married to his mom, and that was, like, five years ago! Why do I have to deal with Josh?
Mr. Horowitz: You divorce wives, not children.

"You divorce wives, not children." I'd watched this movie hundreds of times, yet I'd never processed that hard-hitting line until that flight from New York City to Florida. Sometimes, it takes perspective for us to pay attention, right? Because my new normal mirrored Mr. Horowitz's situation, I finally processed something I had heard so many times. I watched this extremely tough litigator with hardly any patience defend his ex-wife's son like he was his own child even though legally, he no longer was. Once you divorce, you have no more legal rights to your stepchildren. The legal rights prevent you from getting any type of custody of them, which restricts your access, and if you've grown to love your stepbaby like they're your own, that can be heartbreaking and devastating for both you and the child.

Perhaps, if my divorce had been because of financial issues, gambling, poor spending habits, or a genuine case of growing apart, I could imagine that continuing a relationship with my stepdaughter would be easy. I wanted to watch her grow, turn sixteen, go to college and become a lawyer or a surgeon. I wanted to watch her get married and navigate that part of her life. Had my marriage ended for any other reason, I'd have remained in her life. But now what?

I know some people believe that once you've had children with someone, they always have access to your body, but that's just not true. I wasn't cynical or jaded enough about life, men, or humans to believe that something like that was even remotely possible. To be honest, I still don't. I had no control over the decisions they made, but what I did have control over, I dropped the ball on. Looking back, not going through a proper vetting process before marriage and not enforcing proper consequences when the small boundaries were crossed during the marriage led me right into divorce. And as we know, by law, divorcing a parent often means that you're also divorcing your stepchild. Depending on the age of your stepchild at the time of the divorce or separation, in order for you to have a relationship with them, you have to rely on their biological parents to foster it.

A SUPER BLEND

Marie is an adult child of a *super* blended family. That sounds funny, but it's true. Marie doesn't know her biological dad, but the man she knows as her dad has been in her life since she was one year old—and she shares his last name. When she was young, after her baby brother died, her parents divorced. When Marie was twelve, her mother Elaine met Frank. Frank and Elaine married soon after meeting, and Frank became Marie's stepdad. Elaine had two children and Frank had one. Their marriage created a SUPER BLENDED family.

When Marie was sixteen, Elaine and Frank separated for six months. Her mother didn't want her to speak to Frank, but to Marie, this was a strange and difficult task. Frank had been the constant father figure in her life for four to five years. How could she just disconnect? Marie, in her teenage defiance and with a heart full of love for Frank, didn't follow her mom's rule and continued to speak to him anyway. Marie said that despite their separation, Frank called her every day to check on her. She appreciated that he didn't discard her.

It was easy for Frank to remain active with Marie despite the strain in his marriage because he viewed Marie as his daughter. Before my current situation, I don't think I handled separation with a stepchild so well. In my pain, I immediately asked him to leave because I couldn't deal with that level of pain and betrayal and look at him every day. The problem was, my very quick reaction to what he had done did not allow me to think of everyone else it would affect. My bonus baby became collateral damage due to my hasty decision. Now, honestly, we were all casualties of his actions, because betrayal will stick its tentacles into all aspects of your life. And because my bonus baby wasn't biologically mine, our relationship took a huge hit.

One week before I found out about my ex-husband's affair with his COBP, my stepdaughter and I were having one of our in-depth love talks that we had two to three times a year. As I lay across the bottom of her bed, I was able to address the first separation. It had been eighteen months since it happened, and it was the first time that she and I had ever talked about it. Her dad and I had been separated for four months, and I hadn't spoken to my stepdaughter. I have a great respect for children and allow them to believe their parents are superheroes until they get to discover otherwise on their own. I apologized and explained that how I'd handled things was one of the biggest regrets of my life. I discarded her, and I feel contrite about it still. I should've been more like Frank.

I received advice from multiple sources, including a few different licensed therapists, regarding maintaining a relationship with my stepchild while I was separated from her dad. The therapists were looking at my short range mental health due to my distress and none of us were looking through long-range glasses, but the whisper told me not to disconnect from her. The whisper said to separate from my husband, not my stepdaughter. Back then, I did not listen to the whisper and follow my own intuition; I let external sources tell me something that went against my whispers. I should have never taken advice to cut ties with my stepbaby when I separated from her father. It drove a wedge between my stepdaughter and me for over eighteen months. The thing is, I never felt at ease about the decision, but there was so much happening that I did not know how to have a relationship with my young bonus kid without having a relationship with the person that connected us.

Advice is peculiar. Sometimes it's given from a person's experience and perspective. My therapists were not stepparents or stepchildren. That may explain why I never felt as if they understood the totality of what I struggled with. I understand that their immediate concern was me, but perhaps if they would have had personal experiences with being a stepparent or being a stepchild, they would have advised me differently. Although I've since learned a lot, at the time, I took their advice because it felt like the right thing to do.

If an oncologist tells you that you have a mole on your arm that they believe may be malignant, you're going to believe them. Science, along with their observations and experience, are enough to make their hypothesis believable; they don't have to actually have a mole or cancer themselves for you to believe them. Therapy is different. Think about it—when you search for a marriage counselor, you're looking for someone who is or has been married. Hindsight is 20/20, and my clear vision now sees that I should have sought therapy from someone who had been in a blended family at some point in their life, whether in their current marriage or because they grew up in one. My advice to anyone experiencing separation or divorce is: don't throw out the baby with the bathwater!

Whoever you have been to your bonus child throughout the marriage, continue to be that same person. It isn't going to be easy, especially in a situation like mine, or worse—when a baby is born out of an affair! Looking at the child of two people who caused major pain in your life will make you want to jump ship, abort mission, and abandon it all. But love! Love makes you do strange things. I love that little girl too much to transfer my pain to her. She doesn't deserve that at all. All lies find their way out of the depths of dark into the light. One day she will learn what happened, and she will get to decide what to do with that information. But I couldn't do anything to harm her. I will always want to protect her. That's who I have always been to her, and that's who I will always be to her. You must do the same. Be the person you are. Don't make your bonus child suffer for the poor decisions of adults.

Have open, honest conversations about what occurred. It's okay to tell your stepchild that you and their biological parent are going to get a divorce. Children should be handled with care, but not lied to. The discussion, like any conversation with children, should be age-appropriate, but it shouldn't be avoided. I knew that my three-year-old was not going to comprehend much of any of this, of course. My six-year-old and my twelve-year-old bonus daughter, on the other hand, wouldn't only process what was happening but would be greatly affected by this change. The same conversations you'd have to protect your biological cubs, have them when dealing with your stepcubs too. Be honest with all of your children in a gentle way. Simply state the facts of the transition without inserting your feelings about the other parent, no matter which side of the coin you fall on.

Tell the child how you feel. Separation or divorce isn't their fault. Allow them to ask questions and hold space for their emotions, because this will be hard for them too. As I told my bonus child as we lay together in her bed chatting, "No matter where I am, there will always be a bed for you there. I love you, my little boo, forever and always." Always save space for them in your home so that they truly know there is some place for them to come back to. Telling them how you feel goes beyond the moment of the initial announcement. If they're old enough to have a phone or device where you can contact them, send them loving notes and messages letting them know they're on your mind. If you have no access because of their age or circumstances, write them an email once a week and save it in your drafts or print it out for them to read one day when you all are able to reconnect.

Leave the ball in their court. Once they know the truth and the age-appropriate information, you have to allow them to process the information and deal with it. We can't dictate how these children are going to feel.

This is now the second (or third) failed relationship that they've been a part of. Plus, depending on the maturity of their biological parents, you will never know the stories the child is being fed. Pass them the ball and leave it with them. They get to decide. Your heart might break from this, but it isn't something you can force. The child may not choose to have a relationship with you, or their biological parents may not allow you to. You have no control here. I mourn for any pain you feel because of this.

Be open to how they process it. Initially, they may be happy that they "get their parent back" all to themselves. They might think there is hope for reconciliation between their biological parents. They might be angry. The kids are important, and their feelings matter. They have big hearts and big emotions, and situations like this can cause trauma for them.

Take care of your mental health. Do what's right for your mental health. During this painful journey, I prioritized everyone else except for myself. Maybe it's a byproduct of being a mom, but whatever it is, there is nothing like a traumatic event to wake you up and check yourself! No one would benefit from a depleted source, and putting everything and everyone before my own needs was slowly draining me. Take care of yourself, be a little selfish, and put your oxygen mask on first. If you don't get that reference or haven't had the opportunity to fly yet, in the event of decompression, an oxygen mask will automatically appear in front of you in most commercial aircraft. The safety briefing always states:

> To start the flow of oxygen, pull the mask toward you. Place it firmly over your nose and

> mouth, secure the elastic band behind your head, and breathe normally. Although the bag doesn't inflate, oxygen is flowing to the mask. If you're traveling with a child or someone who requires assistance, secure your mask first, and then help the other person. Keep your mask on until a crew member advises you to remove it.

The key to this instruction is this: "If you're traveling with a child or someone who requires assistance, secure your mask first, and then help the other person." When you first hear that instruction, it's quite startling. Why would a parent choose to help themselves before their helpless child? A parent is always supposed to put their child first, so why would the airline industry collectively agree that this was a smart instruction? Well, the purpose of this instruction is quite simple: If you can't breathe, then not only will you die, but so will your child. A quick moment of selfishness—or self-care—will save you and your child. It's hard to be selfish because by definition, it means that a person is "concerned excessively or exclusively with oneself."[23] As a stepparent, you aren't selfish, but in this instance you have to consider your emotions first.

Seek advice from people who have been in your shoes. I never *wanted* to be divorced. But my boundaries were crossed too many times. I always desired peace, because I had grown up in a peaceful home, so not having it felt foreign to me. Even before the affair,

---

23 "Selfish Definition & Meaning," *Merriam-Webster*, accessed September 8, 2024, https://www.merriam-webster.com/dictionary/selfish.

the upheaval around stepparenting was just hard. I'm sure it's a hard journey for most in the beginning, but I dealt with it the entire time. It wasn't until the last six months of the marriage that myself and the COBP were getting along. An eight-year marriage, ninety-six months, and she and I had gotten along for 6% of that time. But I later wondered if it had been real, because during those last six months I learned about their affair, so there's that.

When the proverbial "sh*t hit the fan," I was momentarily stuck. We had just relocated to Manhattan, leaving everything familiar behind in Long Island. My children were in brand-new schools around kids they didn't know. I had just started a new job, and not just any job, either—my *dream* job. I didn't know who to call for advice on how to manage this situation. I didn't know anyone with two small children and a new executive-level job who had successfully managed being divorced. Then a former colleague came to mind. She and her ex-husband had both been each other's second marriage. She was a successful executive who had been through a divorce with two small children. She would become my divorce guru.

Her advice to me when navigating what would be my new life of single motherhood? "Don't be afraid to be selfish right now. It is okay, and your kids will benefit from it." I'm slowly beginning to see what she means. The thing is, when you put yourself first or when you just take care of *you* even a little bit, everyone else benefits. Your mental health is paramount when you're a parent, and especially when you're a stepparent. If you let the parent that you married, the bonus child, or the COBP come first, you won't make it. I *promise* you.

Do not let your partner or the COBP make you feel guilty about it, either! They aren't together anymore, so at some point they, too, decided to be selfish and choose themselves over their relationship! They decided that the family structure, their marriage, their relationship was no longer working, so they decided to depart from it. That is prime selfishness, and it's okay. The reason why it's okay is because in theory, if the relationship is broken, it will eventually break the children. Whatever you need to do to stay sane, you do it! If that means you cannot maintain a relationship with your bonus child right away or ever, that is a choice you need to make.

Don't allow yourself to die with the marriage or the ending of the relationship. Stay alive, by any means necessary. You deserve that, and if you have your own children who rely solely on you, they deserve to breathe and get that oxygen as well. And if you're able to have a relationship with your bonus baby after separation or divorce, go for it.

MAP Title: Put your oxygen mask on and don't throw out the baby with the bathwater.

MAP Legend:

- You don't have to divorce your stepchild.
- Hold physical and emotional space for your stepchild in your life.
- Leave the ball in your stepchild's court.

MAP Directions:

- Would you be okay with your child having a relationship with your ex-spouse?
- Would you want to continue a relationship with my child if our relationship didn't work out?
- Do you let all of your exes have relationships with your children, or do you reserve that only for someone you're married to?

Chapter 11: Why Do I Feel Like I Am in Mourning?

My traditional norm was wildly different from a blended family, and I was not prepared for it. Let's take something as simple as having family dinners. With a blended family, sitting at the dinner table is always so different. Either one of your biological parents can't be there or one of your half-siblings might not always be there. Learning about your ancestors and family dynamics can be vastly different. My nuclear background gave me a naivety when it came to blending with my then-husband and his daughter. I didn't have the experience, knowledge, or tools to deal with the family I married into.

Have you ever tried to make a smoothie with the wrong blender? When I'm making a smoothie, I go through a few steps. When I'm blending spinach or oats, I use the single-serve cup first. Something about that device blends everything so smoothly, and when I'm making smoothies for the kids, if they can chew anything, they don't want it! So, to avoid wasting my precious time and these expensive groceries, I take an extra step just to make sure I know it's right. Once the milk and spinach form a smooth, velvety mixture, I take the single-serve cup off of the blender and take out the big one. I pour the velvety mixture from the small blender into the big one and then I add ice, yogurt, and fruit. The reason why I transfer everything into the large blender is because if I add all of the ingredients to the single-serve cup, everything overflows, and remember, we aren't trying to waste time or these expensive groceries! I used the small blender for the spinach and oats because I've made smoothies without doing that and watched all my hard work and expensive fruit go to waste because kids will just not drink a chunky smoothie. I know to use the large blender because I have made the mistake of putting too many ingredients in the small blender and watching my ingredients end up on the wrong side of the blender—the outside.

The outside . . . that's almost metaphoric, because to be honest, one of the things that feels so sad—one of the feelings you will need to mourn—is feeling like an outsider in your own family. Ask any active stepparent and they will tell you that they sometimes feel like an outsider in their own home. It's a wild dynamic. I believe boundary setting, a loyal spouse, and things being in order can greatly decrease these feelings, but it still exists somewhere in the ether when the COBP isn't a settled human being and wants to come in between your relationship with your stepchild. The bond between you and your biological children is more than likely natural. I'd dare to say that even when you adopt a child from birth, it's natural. My bond with my nieces, nephews, and godchildren is natural. I've known them from birth, and none of their parents intervene in our relationship. Stepparenting, meanwhile, is a beast. In the beginning, nothing feels natural; it is all forced. The moments that are real, natural, true, and loving can be overshadowed by a bitter parent. It sucks.

OUT OF THE MOUTHS OF BABES

Quinn Michael is a five-year-old boy who loves his parents dearly! After a year of dating, Quinn Michael's mom, Monica, introduced him to Harrison, her new companion. Monica and Harrison were in love and planned to get married. But Monica needed to introduce her son to Harrison before she'd entertain saying, "I do." Well, as is any parent's dream, once they finally met Quinn Michael quickly became smitten with Harrison, and Monica was delighted. Monica and Harrison began incorporating him into their quality time, and the three of them were bonding nicely.

One day, Harrison and Monica picked her son up from school. Quinn Michael hugged his mom and they walked to the car holding hands. Harrison stepped out of the car as Quinn Michael was chatting with his mom. Quinn Michael looked up and saw Harrison. He dropped his book bag at his mom's feet, yanked away from his mom's hand, and sprinted toward Harrison while screaming, "HARRISONNNNNN!" It was fair to say that Quinn Michael loved Harrison.

He was quite a talkative little boy, and Monica made sure to never silence this part of him. She never did anything around her son that she wouldn't want on the front page of the *New York Times*, because he'd repeat it. Quinn Michael was this way with everyone, so naturally, when he would go visit with his Dad, he would talk about Harrison and how much fun they had together. One day, Harrison came over Monica's to have dinner with Quinn Michael and Monica. They sat together, prayed, and began to enjoy the dinner that Monica had cooked. Quinn Michael was doing what he does best: chatting away. Harrison went to take a bite of his lasagna and as the fork was entering his mouth, Quinn Michael said, "Harrison, my daddy doesn't like you and he told me to stop talking about you all the time." Harrison dropped his fork and was at a loss for words. Monica could see the pain in Harrison's eyes and replied, "Quinn Michael, that's not very nice to say." He responded, "But he said it, and you told me to always tell the truth." At this point, both Monica and Harrison were silent for what seemed to be an eternity. Quinn Michael continued, "But I told Daddy that Harrison is nice to me and I love him, so oh well. Mommy, today my poop was green." Harrison and Monica busted out laughing and finished eating dinner.

That moment could have easily gone left. Harrison couldn't believe that his feelings could be hurt by a five-year-old. He had lost his appetite and his words. The best thing you can do in a situation like this is manage your expectations! Children can be blunt, brutally honest little creatures, and sometimes the things they say can sting and feel downright mean. Remember that they are children. Even the little ones that are biologically yours will say some things to you that will shock you. Also keep in mind that depending on the stage you've entered in this child's life, they may be feeling levels of confusion, sadness, and trauma from their biological parents no longer being together. Depending on what side of the family you're on, whether you're the parent who chose to walk away from the family or the parent who was left, you have a different family dynamic now, and no matter how you slice it, you got a chunky-ass smoothie. Unless you get the right tools and learn how to deal with it, you're wasting your precious time.

Words will sting. Every time your spouse refers to "their firstborn," you will fill a pang in your stomach. As parents, we can choose to be sensitive about how we speak, especially when we know that the blend is chunky and the ex is the mess left on the counter. As the single person coming into the relationship, it is hard dealing with the mess. I'm a parent now, but I was once a single girl dating a parent. I've come to notice that many women having their first child with someone who already has a kid want their first baby to be the opposite sex of the child that already exists, because they want to be able to say, "This is his first son, his only baby girl, the one that will carry his last name," and so on. When I think about it, I believe it's part of the grieving process. It's the grief that you will never be able to say you had the first child. For a man, the grief can be different. Some have expressed that simply having the child carry another man's last name is difficult for them. Others grieve over the relationship, or lack thereof, that they have with their stepchild. I've had quite a few stepdads tell me that it is hard to bond with their stepchild, where bonding with their biological children is a simple task.

These feelings exist, they are real, and it is okay to mourn something that you may have previously had while growing up or simply longed for: a nuclear family. It is okay that you hate that the woman you love has a child with the last name of a man that you've experienced disrespect from. It is normal that you fantasize that all of your kids, including the bonus kid, came from you and that you didn't have to take into account someone else's moods, schedules, behaviors, and opinions when you parent. It is okay to wish your children had features from both you and the parent that you married. It's okay! Stepparents are silenced from having real feelings because it is always about the kid. The children are important, but you're allowed to have a voice. You no longer have to feel silenced. Your emotions matter. You are a human—you're allowed to have these feelings. For singles in the dating phase, the parent you're dating needs to make you feel important. Although they've experienced things that are new to you, you want to ensure that you feel supported, honored, and loved as you have your firsts.

I have experienced periods of mourning. I mourned not having a traditional family, but it didn't begin until I truly understood what it was like being part of a blended family. I know a major part of my grief came from the lack of boundaries and mess, but I think even if all of that had been healthy, I still would have had some feelings of grief. It was a complex emotion. There were times when I felt sad that my stepdaughter was not present at events. My brother was getting married in Jamaica, and we were so excited because this was our first time traveling internationally as a family of four. We got her passport, booked the tickets, bought dresses, and got a suite. Days before we were supposed to leave to head to our five-star resort to celebrate my brother and his family, the COBP decided her daughter wouldn't attend the wedding for safety reasons on the island. The decision rocked us.

It was a sad moment for my entire family, who had accepted my stepdaughter as their niece, cousin and granddaughter. My heart sank when my four-year-old nephew asked, in the sweetest voice, "Where's my cousin?" Talk about grief! Mourning isn't just about accepting that your family looks different; no, grief also comes from the third party who makes big decisions that affect your entire family. The grief is also buried in moments where the child that you've fallen in love with is not around.

Parents, you may experience grief too. The grief that I experienced as a stepmom is different from my parent grief, but it is still grief nonetheless. Sharing your children is hard, especially after divorce or separation. A year before we got divorced, we attended a friend's gender reveal barbeque. The dad had a child from a previous relationship who was excited to find out if he was going to have a little brother or sister. He didn't care either way. His only concern was his big brother status. He popped the balloon, and the pink confetti went everywhere. He was elated! The look on his face was pure joy.

At the end of the night, his dad and stepmom dropped him off at his mom's house because it was her weekend. As we left the BBQ, he began to cry. He wanted to stay with his dad and continue to bask in the energy of his newfound big brother title. It was so sad to watch. I tried to talk to him, but it didn't help. His dad looked sad, and so did his stepmom. Little did I know that a year later, I'd go from empathizing with him to understanding exactly how he felt. Every time the kids leave, it feels like someone stuck their hand inside of your chest to squeeze your heart. That intense sadness that some parents feel when they send their kid to be with the other parent is grief. There is something different about sending them to their grandparents' home or letting them go with one of your siblings versus watching them drive away with the person you once had a family with. You will grieve that in the beginning. Eventually, like all forms of grief, you will accept it, but expect to experience it.

Hold space for the COBP as well. Just as the parents are mourning having to part ways with their child weekly or biweekly, the COBP is also mourning what was supposed to be *their* traditional family. Most people want to give their kids a two-parent household. It's the standard that we've seen in society, religion, and television shows. The message is clear: a healthy two-parent household is good for the child. Although we are all dealing with a level of loss, we have to allow ourselves to grieve, heal, and move forward. The emotional baggage of grief cannot hold space in any new relationships, so before you move into anything new, *grieve.*

If you're dating and discussing marriage, it's okay to love someone who has a child, and it's okay to be loved if you're someone with a child. If you want to be a married parent, that is a choice that you deserve to make. You deserve to find a good human who will love you and support you as a parent, but they don't deserve any of your baggage. Do not go back out into the dating market if your heart is still reeling from the pain of being left or having to leave your family. You aren't ready. You're carrying emotional baggage, and it doesn't belong at your new address! Heal the things that went wrong as much as you can. Maybe it was all your fault, or perhaps none of it was your fault. Either way, you have to take a little of the hit—you either chose wrong or stayed too long. Whatever it was, heal from it.

As you make the big decision to leap or not to leap into the blender and marry a parent, I urge you to make sure that the parent you consider is mature, loyal, and understanding of who you are and how you feel. It is okay to marry a parent, and if no one has ever told you, let me be the first—and then you share this same sentiment with anyone you know who may be marrying a parent! Your life will be different, as many of your experiences won't be the parent's first. You deserve your moments. If any of this is a first for you, you deserve to have that. Make sure that when you're in the courting stage, this is a dialogue that you openly talk about. If you marry a parent, let them know that even though they have a kid or two that you have never had one, and when you have one, you want it to be a special experience.

A mature parent will give you everything you desire. Do not hesitate to speak up and know that you're normal, and so are your feelings. Go cry, scream, drink some wine, pray—whatever you normally do when you grieve, do it! Grieve it. You're part of a blended family, and your life will be a bit different. It is okay.

MAP Title: Grieve it!

MAP Legend:

- As a parent, you will feel sadness when you separate from your children.
- As a stepparent, you will have to mourn not being the first.
- Mourning traditional families for both singles, parents, and stepparents is normal.

MAP Directions:

- How did you grieve the loss of your relationship?
- How do you feel when your children have to go with your COBP?
- How would you support my firsts (ex: having a baby or getting married)?

Chapter 12: Thy Will Be Done?

Let's close out this book with the most uncomfortable conversation of all: wills and estates. I swear, one of the most dreaded topics is death. Why is the only thing that is sure to happen to all of us so taboo? I guess facing mortality is difficult for most people. It's scary. We begin to assess what we have done, what we have not done yet, and maybe the biggest fear of all is how the demise will occur. Well, guess what? We don't know, and to me, that is comforting!

Let's look at it more pragmatically. When I die, I know my children will be sad, and I prefer that the sadness of my death is the only worry they will have. I want to have all of my personal matters as well as businesses so tightly buttoned up that they inherit what they're supposed to inherit and continue to live their lives comfortably, take over Mama's businesses and properties, and take an actual year to grieve if they want, instead of the five days of bereavement leave that companies give them. Simple. Right? Well, I think through eleven chapters of this book we have figured out together that marrying a parent is everything BUT simple, so let's dive in.

Think about how hard you've worked over your lifetime. Think about the properties you've purchased or plan to purchase, the life insurance you've been paying on monthly, the stocks and 401(k) that your job has been taking money out of your check for, the business you built from the ground up, the diamond ring that your grandmother left you, the farm that you inherited from your Nonna in Italy. Now, imagine all of that going to your COBP or your stepchild's mother or father. OOF. Did that just make you want to vomit? Well, it should! If you die without a will, there is a possibility that something like this can happen. Say an accident happens and your spouse passes at the same time as you. Your spouse has a child living from a previous relationship, and all of your cumulative assets pass to your stepchild. Imagine two years after your accident, your stepchild has an accident and leaves no will, no children, and no siblings. The only surviving beneficiary is your child's other parent, who has been an utter jerk to you for eighteen years. Well . . . guess who inherits everything you left to your stepchild? The COBP. Awful, right?

CRUEL DISINHERITANCE

My friend Emily grew up in one of the most blended families I've ever known. Her mother and father divorced when she was young, and she had two biological siblings from that union. Her father met someone who had four children of her own. They married and had one child together. Things were rocky at first, but eventually they became one big blended family. Emily's biological mother and stepmother became friends, and family events and holidays became a lot easier for my friend, her siblings, her stepsiblings, and the parents. She resides in the house that her biological parents shared, the house she was conceived in, the house that she grew up in. She is now raising her daughter in that house with her spouse. Emily's father always intended for the house to be hers. One day, he called and asked her to sign paperwork that would legally make the house her property. Emily was rushing—trying to get her daughter registered for school—and forgot about it. Not too long after, as life would have it with all of its unexpected twists and turns, Emily's beloved father got sick and passed away. Because there was no will and she didn't get a chance to sign the papers, her stepmother now owns the home. It didn't matter what my friend's dad intended.

THE ASSETS GET DIVIDED

Evette's husband, Tommy, has two grown children from a previous relationship. Evette and Tommy share three children, ages six, two, and eight months. Evette and Tommy live in a state where if you die intestate, without a will, the state will give the first $50,000 of the estate to the surviving spouse, and then everything else has to be split equally amongst the children and the surviving spouse. If Tommy were to die, Evette would split all of Tommy's assets with five children, two of whom are grown women with their own families. This sounds bizarre, but the intestate laws (laws that kick in when there is no will) are archaic and wouldn't put you as the spouse first.

Sarah's mother, Nancy, and her stepfather, Juan, were happily married for thirty years. Sarah had two stepsiblings from her stepfather's previous marriage. Nancy passed when Sarah was in college, but Juan and Sarah's biological father Mike continued to take great care of her, and her dads continued the great friendship that they developed years earlier. When Juan passed away, Sarah was called to participate in the reading of his will. Juan had amassed many properties in NYC and decided to leave his "precious stepbaby," as he wrote in his will, two million-dollar properties. The properties were willed directly to Sarah from Juan when Sarah was a child.

There are many people who marry a parent and leave assets to their bonus children. You can do whatever you'd like, but it should be what *you* want, not what the state says, and definitely not allowing anyone to disinherit your children. If you marry a parent, make sure they are stable, that they have means to take care of themselves, their children, you, and the children that you create together, both while they are here on this earth and when they pass. All parties—the parent, the children, and the person marrying the parent—will have issues if there is no will. The purpose of the will is not to cut anyone out of your will; instead, it is so that you get to choose how your property, assets, and family heirlooms are distributed. Contact an attorney who is experienced in wills and estates, because much like marrying a parent, it will be complex.

MAP Title: Get your will done!

MAP Legend:

- A will is an important part of family planning, especially in a blended family.
- Get a wills and estates lawyer who is well versed in blended families.

MAP Directions:

- What measures have you taken to ensure your children's financial security?
- Have you discussed your will and estate plans with your children or their other parent?
- Is your COTB set to inherit anything in your will?

A FINAL WORD

Look at you! You've made it to the end of the *Marrying ApParent* bootcamp. Congratulations. Use this book to recalibrate your marriage or to make major decisions on whether you will move forward with the person you've been dating.

If you're a single person newly dating someone with a child, you're equipped with conversation starters that will help you to better evaluate your choices. Maybe you've used this roadmap to evaluate your readiness. Some of you have learned that not only are you with an amazing person, but they're also a great co-parent to their COBP and a phenomenal parent to their child. Don't rush—be patient. As the old adage says, "Patience is a virtue." By being virtuous, showing high moral standards, we protect ourselves from being engulfed, flooded, and drawn out to sea in the riptide because our partners did not put out the flags that they knew should have been placed there. Patience allows you to take the steps to truly evaluate the person that you're in a relationship with. You can now properly evaluate their readiness, and yours too! You can either walk away in peace or ride off into the sunset with your future spouse and stepbaby in tow, but in either case you will be prepared!

If you're a parent, you now understand how important it is to set boundaries with your COBP, to have special time with your child, and to put your future spouse first. You understand that if you got stuck on a chapter or have not set the necessary boundaries yet, you're not ready to go back into the dating pool just yet. Remember, I was the single, I was the stepparent, and now I'm the parent, so I get it! Missing companionship and parenting without a partner in the home to tag in when you're tired is hard, but we can't rush into this without making sure we check the boxes, turn the hue of the flags from crimson to emerald, and get in the most peaceful place possible with ourselves, our babies, and our COBP. The whole purpose of what you just went through is to activate your spidey senses. Would *you* date you right now? Do you have things in order so that you can smoothly transition into a relationship with a new person without shaking up your or your child's life too much? It's okay if you're not. Now, you have a tool to use so that you will be.

To my stepparents, how are you doing? Do you feel seen? Do you feel heard? As a fellow stepparent, I hope this book voices our stories. You're in the trenches, but guess what? Sometimes a hard reset is required to function properly. Maybe you see red flags in your marriage, maybe your COBP is giving you hell, or maybe the parent you married is overwhelmed with being the referee or putting too much responsibility on you. Yank the plug from the wall and start all over again. Sit down with your spouse so you can recalibrate. Go through this roadmap again, go get a marriage counselor who specializes in blended families, and get the chunks out so that your blend can be smooth. You got this!

Marrying ApParent is not a cautionary tale. This is not a tool to warn you of danger. Instead, it is getting you ready and prepared to have a long-lasting marriage and the smoothest blend possible with your family. Having a blended family can be beautiful! The way my family embraced my stepdaughter from the first day that they met her just showed that although relationships need boundaries, love has no bounds. I remember the day she dropped her little four-year-old guard down and we fell in love. She is special to me. She always will be, because my love for her is unconditional and boundless. When I married her dad, she gained cousins, aunties, uncles, and a grandma instantly. Being single and becoming an instant parental figure is fun! You get to be a friend and a confidant. Really, it can be motherhood without the "hood," as long as you marry someone who is battle-tested and successfully passes the *Marrying ApParent* bootcamp. When you marry someone healthy and with strong boundaries, your role as a stepparent can be seamless. Being a stepparent can be rewarding.

Finding love as a parent, whether your marriage ended or you were a solo parent from the start, gives your children the opportunity to see romantic love in the household. Being a married parent gives you partnership and companionship and a teammate. It gives your children more family and someone to look up to, and hopefully it gives your COBP someone that they can rely on to stand in the gap on the days that they can't be physically present.

When I handed in my last chapters to my editor, I thought something was missing, but I couldn't put my finger on it. A friend said my *Marrying ApParent* Instagram page could be more positive, so I thought maybe I needed to end this boot camp with flowers, rainbows, and fluff. But after the realness of the last chapter, I just couldn't bring myself to change my views or perspective because it was not meant to be positive or negative; it was meant to be informative.

When I first began writing *Marrying ApParent* in 2018, I interviewed five adult stepchildren because as a stepparent, I wanted to understand how the children in these situations were affected and felt. It was really important not only that I had a voice, but that I fully understood how my actions would ultimately affect my stepdaughter. I was ignorant to this world, but tapping in with people I knew gave me insight into their experiences that they were fully able to articulate since they no longer felt the pressure of taking sides. I touched on those stories a bit but did not fully incorporate them into the book. Their words carried an older perspective, the voice of people with their own families and children who could recall the memories but were no longer being parented, so still I searched for a proper ending.

When Charlamagne tha God appeared on Steven Bartlett's podcast *The Diary of a CEO*, he asked Charlamagne about the current state of politics in the United States. Charlamagne said: "There is nuance to everything."[24] The mental health champion, *New York Times* best-selling author, radio host, TV personality, comedian, and entrepreneur continued by explaining that it's essential to take the time to understand where the other person is coming from. You need to listen to both perspectives, as the only way to truly grasp the reality of a situation is by considering both sides.

[24] "Charlamagne tha God Opens Up About His Depression & Childhood Trauma!" YouTube, posted May 27, 2024, https://www.youtube.com/watch?v=1Rd9Iuxjb5k.

For the very first time, I could see the nuance that Charlamagne mentioned. I became the other side and could fully process "where the other person was coming from." Oddly, it did not change my perspective much. I still believe boundaries are necessary. I still believe stepparents need a voice. And I still believe in the order of things. However, there is one seat that I have never and will never sit in, and that is the seat of the stepchild. The voice of the stepchild is the best way for anyone reading this book to understand how important it is to go into these relationships with caution and knowledge. It can be beautiful when you fall in love as a parent or fall in love with a parent, but you MUST consider that a third party exists. This person, like it or not, will be factored into many of your choices.

INSIGHTS FROM A STEPCHILD

Kayliah is a double stepkid (both parents remarried) and had *so much* insight on the blend, and she stressed the importance of kicking off the relationship with a good introduction. Of all the adult stepchildren that I interviewed, Kayliah's story was the most poignant. At the time of our interview Kayliah was twenty years old, so not only was her perspective fresh, but she was still very actively being parented. Here are Kayliah's thoughts.

- **Don't be offended by titles:** "I really don't think it's that serious unless you treat them that way. As long as you treat everyone the same, the title doesn't matter. It's not that deep." The labels of half-sister or stepsister, stepmom or stepdad aren't negative; they just are. "It's not anything worth being offended over. I thought it was always so weird when I'd introduce or refer to my siblings as my stepsister or my half-sister and an adult would say, [her voice goes into a mocking tone] 'No, that's your sister, that's your sibling!' I explain it this way so that no one gets confused as to why I have four parents, or thinks that these four siblings that I have came from my mom or dad. There is no need to be offended by being called stepsibling. It's okay, I still love them equally and all the same."

- **Explain how life will change:** "I went through an entire shift. I was living with my mom, and then we moved to a new city. We were in a new apartment and I had a new stepdad. I was no longer with my family—it was a big change in my life. There was no explanation. I remember my mom sitting me down and asking me how I felt about moving, and it sounded fun to me. I just thought it meant new things. When we arrived, I was not prepared for it."
- **Your child needs to spend time with their future stepparent:** "If you're going on dates five times a week with your partner, you should include your child in two to three of those dates to prepare them for living with this person every day of their life. A gradual hangout session before you live together is necessary. I do believe it depends on the gender of the parent. I didn't need this so much with my stepmom, because I understood what it was like being a mom to a girl child. I also think I was

more protective of my mom because I lived with her every day, so it felt like a real switch. I wish I could have had dates with them together and some time with him [my stepdad] and I by ourselves."

- **All parents must agree on the parenting style:** "I was ten when we became a blended family. So before my stepdad, it was just me and my mom. The best way is for the parent (mom or dad) to be the main disciplinarian. The stepparent is allowed to reprimand their stepchild, but if I had to break it down into percentages, the stepparent should be doing 30% and the parent should be doing 70% of the discipline."
- **Talk about how you want to raise your children:** "It's important for the single to ask the parent, 'How do you want us to raise your child?' There is one thing to have a conversation about how we want to raise the children that we share, but the single person needs to ask the parent about their current parenting style. You shouldn't reprimand the child more than their biological parent. You shouldn't try to raise a child when it's not in your parenting style." Questions Kayliah suggested: Are you okay with me reprimanding your child? If you're okay with me reprimanding her, how? How do I fit into this equation?
- **Connect with your stepchild beyond the finances:** "You have to show up for your children financially. It's not a prize or a badge of honor. Making your child feel like providing a

roof over their head equates to emotional support and love isn't fair. You don't expect anything back from your biological child, so why is there an expectation that you're going to get something back from your stepchild? Support is great, but I also need emotional stability. Just because you bought the food doesn't mean that our relationship is perfect now."

- **Carve out quality time:** "I had one-on-one time with my mom, but I always wanted more. I was used to it being just us. We got some good one-on-one time. As I got older, it became harder because I wasn't as transparent with my mom. Sometimes I just felt like I needed more time."
- **Get to know your stepchild:** "Don't raise me like I'm some random child. My stepdad was raising me based on how he was raised instead of raising me in the way I needed to be raised. My mind wasn't mischievous. I think if he knew me better, it would have been better."

As we closed out, I said to Kayliah, "You're old enough to give grace, but young enough to remember how you felt in the moment." Kayliah loudly agreed, "YES! That's exactly how I'd describe it." Not only is it important for a stepparent to get to know their stepchild, but it's also very important for a child to learn their stepparent. This is something that comes with age. Hearts can be mended, relationships can be fixed, and sometimes we learn that our ways as a child can change as we get to understand life more.

We need to consider how our children might be feeling, their perspectives, and how they're interpreting these blends. This hour-long interview taught me so much that I wish I'd known before becoming a stepmom. Kayliah's thoughts and all of the interviews from all of the lovely couples, singles, parents and stepparents (stories that made these pages and those that didn't) along with my very own experience have given me so much insight on marrying a parent, and my hope is that has done the same for you.

ACKNOWLEDGEMENTS

I am deeply grateful to the incredible individuals who supported me throughout the journey of writing this book. To my Mommy, thank you for allowing me to be uncomfortably vulnerable and for your unconditional love. To my Daddy in heaven, thank you for the inheritance of hustle and ambition. To my Sisters, Monk and Kimbo, thank you for encouraging my shenanigans and also always being so proud of me. To my baby brother, E, thank you for your creativity, insight, guidance and patience. To my K Cup, thank you for the help and battery you always put in my back and the title of Harriet Tubman. To all of my family and friends, your unwavering belief in me kept my spirits high and my focus sharp. Special thanks to my book coach and editor, Taiia Smart Young, for your tireless efforts in bringing out the best in my work and your continued encouragement, which helped me realize that I AM an author. To my creative director and marketing guru, Eric Martin, Jr., I am not sure that thank you is enough. To my literary lawyer, Denise Gibbon, thank you for your insight, understanding, and laughs. To the many people who shared their stories with me, your courage and honesty have enriched these pages beyond measure. To my forever bonus baby, I love you, Munchkin. Finally, to my readers—thank you for allowing me to be a part of your journey. This book is for you.

ABOUT THE AUTHOR

Erica Grace is an advocate. She is a commercial, technology, and entertainment lawyer, an adjunct professor, and the founder of Marrying ApParent, a platform created to support stepparents and people who are considering marrying a parent. Through her own lived experience and extensive interviews with single parents, stepparents, singles, and adults who were raised as stepchildren, Erica has gathered valuable insights on the experience of dating and marrying a parent.

Erica was born and raised in Queens, NY, and currently lives in NYC with her two beautiful children, Lucas and Sloan.

Master the Art of Dating Someone with Kids

Are you navigating the complexities of dating or marrying someone with children? Struggling to find balance and harmony with your partner? Unsure how to make time for yourself while juggling your responsibilities as a single parent? *Marrying ApParent* by Erica Grace is more than just a book—it's your roadmap to relationship success.

Learn how to build a strong, loving connection with your partner!

Book Erica for coaching sessions or speaking engagements and learn how to transform your challenges into opportunities for growth and love. With her guidance, you'll gain the confidence and wisdom to navigate the most challenging aspects of marrying a parent and emerge stronger than ever.

Contact Erica Grace for coaching and speaking opportunities at www.marryingapparent.com.